YOUTH MINISTRY in SMALL CHURCHES

By Rick Chromey

Group
Books

Loveland, Colorado

and our R.E.A.L. Guarantee to you.

Every Group resource incorporates our R.E.A.L. approach to ministry—a unique philosophy that results in long-term retention and life transformation. It's ministry that's:

Relational
Because student-to-student interaction enhances learning and builds Christian friendships.

Applicable
Because the aim of Christian education is to be both the hearers and doers of the Word.

Experiential
Because what students experience sticks with them up to 9 times longer than what they simply hear or read.

Learner-based
Because students learn more and retain it longer when the process is designed according to how they learn best.

This is EARL. He's R.E.A.L. mixed up. (Get it?)

Youth Ministry in Small Churches
Copyright © 1990 by Rick Chromey

Credits
Edited by Eugene C. Roehlkepartain
Cover and book designed by Judy Atwood Bienick
Cover photo by David Priest

Scripture quotations are from the Holy Bible, New International Version. Copyright © 1973, 1978, 1984 International Bible Society. Used by permission of Zondervan Bible Publishers.

Library of Congress Cataloging-in-Publication Data
Chromey, Rick
    Youth ministry in small churches / by Rick Chromey.
    p.   cm.
    ISBN 0-931529-76-X
    1.   Church work with youth—United States.   2. Small churches—United States
    I.   Title
    BV4447.C485   1989
    259'.23—dc20
20   19   18   17   16   15   05   04   03   02   01
Printed in the United States of America.

VIsit our Web site: **www.grouppublishing.com**

Dedication

To Patti and Becky.
I love you.

Acknowledgments

I could never have shared any of the ideas, thoughts and experiences in this book without the support, encouragement and prodding from the following people:

• First of all, my wife Patti. You were ever patient despite late-night manuscript revisions, appeals for silence and suffering as a "writer's widow." I love you.

• Gene Roehlkepartain (my editor) and the staff of Group Books. You saw the importance of small church youth ministry and had the faith to enlist a fledgling writer to address the need.

• My former church secretary, Marilyn Abbott. You faithfully and painstakingly corrected poor grammar and misspellings as you proofread the manuscript. You're more than "staff"; you're a friend!

I also want to offer a special thanks to the following churches: First Christian Church, Blair, Nebraska; Oakley Christian Church, Oakley, Kansas; Felicity Church of Christ, Felicity, Ohio; New Vienna Church of Christ, New Vienna, Ohio; and Madeira Church of Christ, Cincinnati, Ohio. You hired me in faith, shared your lives with me, and taught me youth ministry. Thanks for the memories.

Contents

Why I Wrote This Book

J erry Richards recently agreed to lead the youth ministry program at his church. He won't get paid, but sometimes it will feel like a full-time job.

Even in a small church, youth ministry is a time-consuming responsibility. There are programs to lead, plans to make, special events to prepare, budgets to submit, volunteers to find, counseling to do and dozens of other things to take care of.

And Jerry won't have much to guide him.

His first task is to prepare to teach Sunday school. He pulls out the curriculum and reads the lesson. "To begin this lesson," he reads, "divide your class into five groups and discuss . . ." He doesn't bother with the rest of the sentence. His group only has four kids.

Of course, this won't be the only time Jerry feels frustrated. As he looks at the many youth ministry resources available today, he'll discover few of them deal with his situation. There just isn't much out there for Jerry and his small church youth ministry.

Few Resources

I wrote *Youth Ministry in Small Churches* for youth workers like Jerry. The thought of writing the book first occurred to me when I was working in a small church near Cincinnati, Ohio. I had vainly searched Christian bookstores for resources. I found a few. But none addressed my needs as a small church youth minister.

It's ironic that so few resources are available for small churches. According to church consultant, Lyle Schaller, the average Protestant congregation in North America has fewer than 40 people in worship on a Sunday morning. Indeed, a quarter of all churches have fewer than 35 people in attendance, and half have fewer than 75.[1]

Thus, most churches are small churches—congregations with fewer than 150 in worship on Sundays. And experts have discovered small churches have unique dynamics that affect all areas of youth ministry. Yet there are few resources for these churches' youth ministries.

Collected Ideas

I realized other small church youth workers might benefit from what I have learned—through trial and error—in several small churches. This book is a collection of the ideas I've gathered and used through several years of youth ministry. The book includes:

• insights to help you understand the frustrations, opportunities and dynamics of youth ministry in small churches;

• practical ideas for designing your ministry to fit your situation;

• suggestions for dealing with the problems that often arise in small churches over budgets and volunteers;

• information on pooling resources with other small churches in your community; and

• encouragement and support to help with the personal stresses you feel in your ministry—whether you're a volunteer or professional youth worker.

A Personal Note

As I wrote this book, I began feeling God leading me back to a small church after serving in a larger congregation for a short time. Not that my larger suburban church youth ministry wasn't successful. I just missed the small church. I missed the feel of "family." I missed the opportunity to touch kids' lives individually.

I recently returned to a smaller church in eastern Kansas. So I'm in the same position you are. Like you, I'm challenging the church to give more money to the youth budget. I'm combing the church directory for volunteers. I'm experiencing the same frustrations of apathy and low attendance that you experience. I have to adapt, create and change programming ideas—just like you do.

So don't think of *Youth Ministry in Small Churches* as a bottle of medicine that will cure all your ills. What worked for me in some places may not work for you—or for me in my new church. What has bombed with me may be your best program.

Instead, think of this book as a spark plug to get you excited about the possibilities in your youth group—even if you just have one group member. I hope the book will "jump start" you to a deeper and more effective ministry. Sure, you'll find lots of ideas. But adapt the ideas to fit your group and your church.

Read the book. Use its ideas. Make it work for you in your small church. But remember, you won't find success by reading a book. True success in your ministry involves staying faithful to Jesus Christ and the abilities he has given you. If you do that, your ministry will succeed. That success may not show in numbers, but Christ will reward your faithful efforts.

Endnotes

[1] Lyle Schaller, *The Small Church is Different!* (Nashville, TN: Abingdon Press, 1982) 9-11.

CHAPTER 1

Problems and Possibilities

I'll never forget walking into the musty church basement that first Sunday morning. I was a college sophomore, and this was my first youth ministry job.

The search committee had assured me the church had "several good prospects" for the youth program. So expecting the best, I came with 15 copies of well-done handouts that I'd spent most of Saturday afternoon typing, photocopying and stapling.

Then people started to arrive. The pastor and several younger children said "hi" as they went to their classes. Some adults stopped by. One elderly woman chatted about the weather. A man who murmured his name handed me a piping-hot cup of coffee. I'd already forgotten his name before he scooted down the hall to his class.

But no teenagers.

I started to worry. Then a young man about 16 walked in, arguing with a slightly younger girl who turned out to be his sister. Aha! The kids were just a little late. They'd start coming now.

But they didn't. My Sunday school class consisted of me, David and Peggy—and Greg and Angie, who came halfway through the lesson.

Welcome to youth ministry in a small church, I thought.

All those college courses hadn't taught me how to minister to this youth group of four—in a church with no youth ministry budget.

Despite my initial frustration, we pulled a youth group together. We started weekly meetings called BYG (pronounced "big") for Blair Youth Group.

The acronym fit my dreams. Everything around me said that big was better. If your group was getting bigger, you were succeeding. I bought the idea and did all that I could to make the youth group bigger and better.

By this standard, I did well. Before long, Kurt and Mark joined the group to form a core. Each Sunday night, new kids showed up. Attendance at BYG meetings exploded to 15— even 20—teenagers! I beamed as I presented monthly reports— seasoned with carefully chosen statistics—to the church board. I even began to boast that the youth group would reach the half-century mark within one year. Parents applauded. Church leaders smiled. Kids kept coming.

But then attendance peaked around 18. The group stopped growing. No matter what I did, I couldn't attract more kids.

Feeling that somehow I was no longer successful, I grew frustrated. I took a summer youth ministry job in another state. The growing church averaged around 150 every Sunday in a town of around 2,000. I discovered the challenge of doing youth ministry in a town with only one pizza joint.

Upon college graduation, I headed for the city. The ministry was tough and lonely. Within weeks of being hired, I found myself depressed and—for the first time—hating youth ministry. Even though the youth group was growing, I felt little satisfaction. I began to realize that numbers didn't equal success. After three grueling months, I submitted my resignation and took a break from youth ministry. I needed time to reflect and put myself back together.

Two months later, I became a weekend youth minister in a small Ohio town. The kids in the church were strong—even though there were only five or six of them. What was different, though, was that I no longer saw these small numbers as challenges to overcome. Rather, they were kids who deserved and needed a strong youth ministry—no matter what size.

I had learned through my experiences that a small church needn't have big numbers to succeed. Big isn't always better.

•　•　•

I've come a long way since I stepped nervously into that small church basement as a college sophomore. Despite the disappointments and mistakes, those first churches taught me youth ministry. And through those experiences, I discovered both the frustrations and the opportunities of small church youth ministry.

Transforming Problems

It's 5 p.m. Sunday. Sue paces just outside the church door, anxiously awaiting tonight's kick-off for a series of youth group meetings.

Sue has advertised, announced, pleaded and pushed to make the event a big success. She even managed to rent a feature film—a monumental feat in itself. Of course, she had spent most of a recent church board meeting explaining why the church should have this movie. It was expensive—really expensive for a small church.

Now the time of reckoning.

It's 5:10. Still no kids. Sue starts getting nervous. What if no one shows up?

As her mind spins, she sees Nicholette and Joanie round-ing the corner. Everyone's just late, Sue reasons as she sighs in relief. Now they're coming.

In welcoming the two, she asks them where everyone else is. "Haven't you heard?" Joanie asks. "The Central High guys won the basketball semi-finals last night. So Mr. Johnson called an emergency band and pep squad practice to be ready for the big game tomorrow night."

"Great. Just great," Sue mumbles sarcastically. She knows that most of her youth group members are active in the band.

Everyone else—save Nicholette and Joanie—is in the pep squad.

Suddenly, at 5:20, the door flings open. It's Jeff, a trumpet player.

"Thought you had practice tonight," Sue says.

"Yeah. But I know this film's important," Jeff replies.

"Well, have a seat. Guess it'll be the four of us."

Sue tries to put a good face on the event, but she's crushed. As the projector shows the movie, faces of missing group members flash through the youth leader's mind. She'd planned for 20, and only three showed up. Where had she failed?

Sue's situation typifies the frustrations of small church youth ministry. Sometimes it feels like nothing works—no matter how hard you try. Let's look at some of the frustrations of small church youth ministry and discover creative ways to turn problems into possibilities.

Lack of money—Most youth ministers—regardless of church size—feel the frustration of limited youth ministry budgets. Yet the frustration intensifies in small churches, which may have trouble paying heating bills, let alone budgeting for special programming. And, unfortunately, youth ministry usually falls under "special programming."

A lack of funds can cripple a youth ministry. Because the budget is small, the youth group has to raise money for every activity. And church leaders feel guilty they can't do more for the youth program. The result is frustration and discouragement.

Few small churches will ever have youth ministry budgets that match big-church budgets. The challenge, then, is to use limited resources in creative ways. You may not be able to take overseas mission trips. But even the smallest church can organize a food drive for local hunger needs.

Your six-member youth group will probably never rent the plush retreat facilities that large youth groups can. But your group of six can retreat to dozens of less-obvious places. A great place for a small youth group retreat is a motel. For around $10 per person, you can have comfortable rooms (with such great extras as hot showers, color television, clean towels and maybe a swimming pool!).

Most churches start supporting the youth program modestly. Randy, a part-time youth minister in Oregon, got his church to create its first youth ministry budget. That might not sound unusual, but it was. Randy's church didn't even have its own budget. However, Randy strongly believed the church could and should support the youth program. So he challenged church leaders to provide $10 per week for youth ministry. It became the seed for important ministries.

Lack of volunteers—When I served a church in a farming community, I had trouble finding youth ministry volunteers. Church members lived by the "farm work ethic": You work hard all week, but Sunday is a day of rest.

They wouldn't break their axiom except in an emergency. Such a philosophy created havoc for the youth program. Since I was a weekend youth minister, I had to design my program for just two days a week. Saturday was the best time for activities, visitation, planning and publicity. That left Sunday for youth group meetings.

In order to have a program for all ages (first through 12th grade), our youth groups began at 3 p.m., when the elementary group met. Then an hour and a half later, the younger kids left as the junior and senior highers arrived. Their meeting lasted until the evening service.

To stay on schedule, I'd eat a quick lunch at a nearby restaurant after morning worship and skip supper altogether. After the evening service, I'd drive back to town (an hour away), not getting home until 9 or 10 p.m. It was exhausting.

So I went looking for adult help for both programs. As hard as I tried, I could recruit only a few volunteers—and they were often unreliable.

It was me—or nobody. But then I had an idea. Why not use the teenagers as volunteers in the elementary group? The older kids could lead games, teach lessons and pass out refreshments. What had been a problem became a possibility. An obstacle became an opportunity to develop youth leadership.

Lack of group members—Probably the biggest frustration in small church youth ministry is the natural lack of numbers. I say "natural" because a small church body has, by definition, a limited number of families with teenagers. That means a small church will generally have a small youth group.

How can we respond to this problem? Remember Sue, whose big film night failed because of an unexpected band rehearsal? She certainly knew the frustration of small numbers. We left her sitting in the back of the room counting empty chairs. "How am I going to explain this to the church board?" she kept asking herself. "They couldn't believe I wanted to pay those bucks for this film in the first place. I'll hear about this one."

An hour later the film ended. As Nicholette flipped on the lights and Sue waited for the film's impact to sink in, Jeff broke the silence: "I'm starved!"

At first Sue was angry. Had no one caught the film's important message? Were these kids completely insensitive?

But Sue thought quickly. "Jeff, that's a great idea!" she blurted out. "Let's go over to Papa's Pizza Place and order a big one. My treat."

Jeff looked at Nicholette. Nicholette looked at Joanie. Joanie looked at Jeff.

"Are you serious?" Nicholette asked, not quite sure how to take the proposal.

"Totally serious," Sue responded. "But I'd like to talk about the film while we're waiting, okay?"

That night's conversation was more meaningful than any program Sue had ever planned. What appeared to be a disastrous situation became a turning point in Sue's ministry. Relationships became more important than rigid ruts of tradition. Sue could never have taken 20 out for pizza. But she could take three.

Small church youth groups may not have many members, but they can be glowing successes. If these groups worry about numbers, they only hurt themselves. Counting kids isn't as important as making kids count.

Lack of enthusiasm—Apathy kills youth groups. Small youth groups aren't necessarily apathetic. Apathy is a slow-spreading disease that begins with an attitude and spreads to a mind-set. Often it's caught by apathetic adults who aren't concerned about teenagers. The disease spreads—unless it's stopped.

We shouldn't shrug off apathy, but we shouldn't be overly afraid of it either. When a youth group I served started becoming apathetic, I planned an Apathy Party. We spent a whole hour doing the dullest and most boring things imaginable. We read to each other . . . from the dictionary . . . in monotone. We held a yawning contest. Then we capped off the hour by watching old home movies of people no one knew. It was the longest hour of those kids' lives!

Then I closed the meeting by talking about how apathy can kill a youth group. The experience sparked a great discussion—and changed the group's outlook. By giving the problem to the group instead of trying to solve it myself, I began the healing process.

Lack of time—As a youth minister, I've been asked to direct youth choirs, oversee summer Bible school programs, serve as Christian education director, organize junior worship hours and even edit the church newsletter. It seems that any job no one else wants ends up in the youth minister's "in" box.

A large church may have a professional staff with a full-time person for each program. But small churches can't afford such luxury. Instead, church staff members often do a dozen different jobs when they were only hired for a couple. And volunteers aren't asked to do youth ministry only; people also want them to teach Sunday school, sing in the choir, serve on church committees, arrange flowers for the sanctuary and do a vast assortment of other tasks.

I remember a particularly demanding week. It was Vacation Bible School week, and I was the director. My wife, Patti, was also involved in the program, but she worked all day in Cincinnati—an hour away.

The week seemed endless. I arrived at the church at 8 a.m. and worked until 4 p.m. Then I drove into Cincinnati to pick up Patti. We'd grab a "McSupper" as we wove through rush-hour traffic in time for evening activities. Then when it was all over, we'd head home to bed around midnight. The sleep was welcome, but the next morning's 6 a.m. alarm wasn't.

I never solved my VBS schedule problem. But what I learned through that and other small church experiences was the need to set personal and professional priorities. I determined that God and family are more important than church work. As a result, if a conflict occurs over whether I should attend an extra church meeting or spend time with my family, my inclination is to spend time with my family—particularly if I haven't done so for several days.

I also learned to set priorities at work.

One way I did this was to stop "majoring on the minors." I stopped doing jobs I could delegate—especially those I could delegate to young people. When I was asked to give a devotional for the Senior Saints' luncheon, I recommended a teenager. When I needed to file a stack of magazines, I asked a youth group member to help. In both cases, the kids were delighted.

When you stop doing things someone else can do, you'll have time to do things that require your expertise.

Lack of contentment—A final problem in small church youth ministry is perhaps the greatest: competition. Small churches can become obsessed with the desire to grow in numbers.

I was caught in the mistaken notion that big is better—that you measure youth ministry success by the chairs you fill. I believed a successful youth minister would make a youth group double or triple in size.

However, while numerical growth may be the natural outcome of a program that meets kids' needs, it shouldn't be the focus. Jesus challenged his followers to "make" disciples, not "count" them (Matthew 28:19).

When small church youth workers shift their focus from bigger numbers and polished meetings to personal relationships and spiritual growth, their perspectives change. They discover you can be both small and successful.

Andrew and Margaret are volunteer youth leaders for a small church in Colorado. By the numbers standard, their ministry is anything but successful. Sometimes they only have two or three kids in Sunday school and youth group meetings.

But 15-year-old Martha's story will help you understand how successful Andrew and Margaret really are as youth ministers. Martha comes from a single-parent family, and her mom offers her little support. In fact, Martha essentially takes care of the whole family.

When Martha started coming to church, she was a misfit. She hadn't developed the social skills of most kids her age, so she had trouble making friends. And she knew nothing about the Bible, the Christian faith or the church.

Andrew and Margaret reached out to Martha. They affirmed her, encouraged her and taught her. She became a Christian and, after a couple of years, an active youth group leader. She invited her friends to come to church with her. And the whole congregation watched this teenager with low self-esteem and little motivation blossom into a growing Christian.

Andrew and Margaret may not appear to be successful to many people. Neither has great charisma or youth ministry training. But their ministry has helped kids like Martha—who don't seem to fit anywhere else—find faith and hope in life.

Celebrating the Possibilities

While small church youth ministry has its problems and frustrations, it also has joys and possibilities. I love working in small churches for a number of reasons:

Opportunities to create "family"—There's something special about knowing everyone in a worship service. Somehow the hugs mean more, the handshakes last longer, and the smiles go further. Granted, some small churches have lost this feeling. Yet many small churches know how to make someone welcome. They know "family" is important.

Lee was a 14-year-old who often did things awkwardly and wrong. Tragically, most kids rejected him. At home his alcoholic father frequently beat him.

Lee considered himself a failure.

Then one night Lee walked into a youth group meeting.

Despite Lee's reputation, the small church youth group reached out. Lee began going to church regularly and found the congregation was also willing to include him. Through that church Lee found family, even though his home life was lousy. He found acceptance, even though he endured ridicule at school.

Lee might have gotten lost in a large church youth group. But through the small church family, Lee found a home.

Opportunities for youth involvement—Most small churches rely on volunteers to fulfill the church's ministries. And because the congregations are small, everyone has to participate.

While some people complain there's always too much to do, being small creates an ideal setting for getting kids involved. Young people can lead worship services, do special music, visit shut-ins, take up offerings, pass out bulletins, serve on church committees—or get involved in virtually any ministry.

Small churches can utilize teenagers' gifts. Matthew was an ordinary kid. He couldn't sing, so he didn't join the choir. He was a poor reader, so he never volunteered to read scripture in morning worship. In fact, most people didn't think Matthew had much of a future.

But the pastor knew differently. Matthew was brilliant in one area: electronics. He'd spend hours fixing broken radios or patching together broken "boom boxes." So the pastor asked Matthew if he'd be interested in operating the church sound system.

That was 10 years ago. Today, Matthew is a missionary in Brazil responsible for maintaining mission equipment. He still can't sing a lick, but his mechanical and electronics abilities make him a valuable asset on the mission field. All because a pastor saw a gift and discovered a way to use it.

Opportunities for personal contact—Perhaps the greatest joy in working with a small church youth group is touching individual kids. The opportunity to hear their hurts, joys, frustrations, triumphs and fears gives vigor and meaning to ministry. Large church youth ministers envy the personal contact possible in a small church.

The kids benefit as well.

Maria went to a large church youth group. She never missed the group's terrific meetings and blockbuster outings.

Then Maria got sick and did miss youth group. She even was in the hospital for a couple of days. Youth group members didn't notice.

A month or so later, Maria bumped into Juan at the supermarket. Juan began telling her about his youth group. He said it was small, but good. Maria decided to see for herself.

Maria went with Juan to youth group the next week. When she walked into the two-room church building where the group gathered, her mouth dropped open. Juan wasn't kidding about the size—five kids, to be exact.

But her discomfort vanished as Juan introduced her to other group members. Within minutes, she knew everyone's name. She had never known everyone in her youth group.

That particular meeting, the kids were planning an upcoming youth service. Would Maria like to participate? She said she could play flute a little and would enjoy playing in church. The leader added her solo to the service. The rest of the meeting included group-building activities and a sharing time in which kids affirmed each other.

Maria never went back to the other youth group. When the large church youth minister noticed Maria's absence a month later, he called to check on her. She explained she was going to a smaller church because she fit in better and they cared about her. He said he was sorry and would miss her. But he never called again.

Funny thing, though. Maria missed the second youth group meeting at the small church. She had told the group she was going to be out of town. When she got home late that Sunday night, Maria found a "Welcome Home . . . We Missed You!" banner on her front door with a personal note from each youth group member.

Both groups had strong content and activities, but only the small group made Maria feel special. The group needed her. And she needed the group.

Reaping the Rewards

As you can see, small church youth ministry can have a tremendous impact on young people. Unfortunately, small churches, small youth groups and small church youth leaders easily become discouraged about the problems and frustrations they face.

This book presents creative ways to overcome the problems of youth ministry in small churches. It examines the frustrations, but it doesn't dwell on them. Instead, it opens up the possibilities for rewarding and effective ministries in small churches. Among other things, you'll discover:

- how to move your group from apathy to enthusiasm;
- how to develop a well-rounded ministry with just a few kids;
- how to get kids actively involved in your church and youth ministry leadership;
- how to find and recruit effective volunteers in a small church;
- how to get funding for your ministry;
- how to network with other small churches in your community; and
- how to maintain a balance between your ministry and your personal life.

In the process, I hope you'll discover the joy of working in small churches. The problems won't go away, and you'll always experience some of the frustrations. But you'll also discover the tremendous possibilities in the ministry God has set before you.

CHAPTER 2

What's Different About the Small Church?

Do this exercise:
● Take two sheets of paper. On one, write "Small Churches I've Been In." On the other, write "Large Churches I've Been In."

● On the left side of each page, write the names of all the churches that fit the heading.

● Next to each church, write your impressions of the church. What struck you most about it? How did you feel? What were the church's strengths and weaknesses?

● After you've jotted notes about each church, compare the two sheets. What do you notice? Do the small churches share many characteristics? the large churches?

● ● ●

If your experiences are typical, the two sheets would be quite different. Some of the differences would be obvious: Small churches don't have as many people as large churches. But other differences would be more subtle. They'd deal with the churches' dynamics, perspectives and priorities.

People who study congregation dynamics find dramatic differences between large and small churches. One expert, Lyle Schaller, focuses on the differences in his book *The Small Church Is Different!* He writes: "The large church is not an enlarged version of the small congregation, and the small-membership church is not a miniature replica of the big church . . .They are almost as different from one another as a village is unlike a large central city."[1]

This chapter focuses on unique small church characteristics identified by Schaller. While Schaller identifies 20 characteristics, this book expands on eight that seem particularly relevant for youth ministry.[2]

The Small Church Is Relational

My fondest memories of my small "home" church in Montana are the monthly fellowship dinners. Disregarding subzero December temperatures or sultry summer sun, everyone showed up. Afterward, kids played Hide-and-Seek while the adults talked away the afternoon.

We were a family.

Relationships make small churches different. Everybody knows everybody. People know and meet each other's needs. When a tragedy occurs, the whole church weeps. When something great happens, the whole congregation rejoices.

Large churches rarely create such an atmosphere through the whole congregation. You may attend a large church regularly for months and still be addressed as a visitor. Potluck dinners may work in larger churches, but not with the ease and simplicity of a small church. When large churches create intimacy, it's usually in small cells—not across the whole congregation.

Close relationships are a key benefit of small church youth ministry. In a world becoming more and more depersonalized, young people seek the intimacy of a small group where they're known and important.

But this close community can also be a problem if it creates a closed group that doesn't welcome newcomers.

You've probably visited a small church that seemed cold and unfriendly, but everyone kept talking about what a friendly church it was. You were an outsider, so you didn't feel the warmth of the inner circle.

The Small Church Is Tough

Juanita is a youth leader in a small Texas church. She's caught in a battle between the church's leadership—which believes the youth program, though small, is on the right track—and a small group of adults who want the church to change its youth ministry philosophy.

The conflict has grown into a crisis. Ten families have left the church—taking their offerings with them. The church is left with a major budget deficit and a smaller youth group.

But the church members have pulled together to hire a consultant to help them resolve the problem. Instead of giving up and going to another church, the committed members have decided to stick together through the tough time.

As this story illustrates, small churches are resilient. A crisis comes, and the church pulls together to weather the storm. The pastor may resign, but weekly attendance will remain relatively steady. In contrast, if a large church loses its pastor, dozens—if not hundreds—of people might leave the church.

Much of this toughness comes because members are highly committed to the church. It's their church, and they won't let a temporary crisis destroy what they've worked so hard to create. In large churches, members who don't feel strong ownership in the church might leave for more comfortable churches.

Small churches' resilience and commitment create a firm context for youth ministry. When the youth program has difficulty attracting kids, church members work together to support the leaders and to find ways to reach more teenagers.

The same toughness and commitment shows in active youth group members. They, too, have strong ownership in the youth group. So leaders know they can count on those kids even when problems arise.

The Small Church Is a Volunteer Organization

In most large churches, if you need something done you hire someone. Need to attract more young people? Then hire a youth minister. Want to have midweek church-fellowship meals? Hire a cook. The larger a church becomes, the more it hires staff for leadership positions.

Small churches can't afford large staffs. Often the only paid person is the pastor—who may only be part-time. Other small churches may pay part-time organists, choir leaders or janitors. So the church relies on laypeople to lead most of its ministries, including youth ministry.

Working with volunteer leaders creates unique dynamics. It's harder to hold volunteers accountable when something goes wrong. Often volunteers don't have the training and skills a professional might have. And since volunteers have other jobs and responsibilities, their time for church leadership may be limited.

Volunteer leadership also has advantages. Because members of small churches generally know each other well, they're more aware of needs and dynamics in the community than is a staff member who's not from the community. Longtime members also know what resources are available locally, and they know who to turn to when particular needs arise.

Small churches help members use their gifts in God's service. In a small church there's a task for everyone. As Gunnar Hoglund writes in Eternity magazine, "Many people with talent vegetate in large church membership rolls, never enjoying the sweat and tears of working on a church program."[3]

In youth ministry, volunteer leadership has both advantages and disadvantages. An important advantage is continuity. Youth ministers tend to change churches regularly, but committed laypeople don't. Thus volunteer leaders develop long-term relationships with young people. They may remember when a teenager was born, and they often stay in touch with teenagers long after they leave the youth group. And when volunteer youth ministry leadership changes, the kids already know the new leaders.

A disadvantage is that laypeople usually don't have the training and experience professional youth workers do. Thus small church youth leaders sometimes struggle independently to develop programs for which several strong models have already been developed. This disadvantage can be overcome by using resources and training events available for youth ministry volunteers.

The Small Church Cares More for People Than for Performance

In his book *Activating Leadership in the Small Church*, Steve Burt tells about preaching in a Maine church with a 92-year-old organist. She was the oldest active organist in the state and she was also quite deaf. Burt writes:

> During my pastoral prayer I must have made some sort of ambiguous gesture, because she began to play the *Gloria Patri* while I was still speaking. People were on their feet in a flash, singing the *Gloria* and chuckling quietly at my plight. Later when I announced Hymn 84, she started playing a different hymn and everyone had to play "Name That Tune" until they could figure out a little of it, look it up in the index, and turn to the new hymn. But the congregation did it with graciousness, good humor, and patience just as they had done for week after week. They were blessed with a strong sense of people priority.[4]

This same dynamic applies to youth ministry. The church and the youth group members don't demand polished programs and precise publicity. What's much more important is that kids are included and relationships are formed.

People are more important than programs. Youth group members can be active worship leaders in small churches because the members are more interested in supporting Nancy and Ian—who want to be ministers someday—than in hearing a perfect 17-minute, three point sermon with provocative insights, humorous stories and practical applications.

So Rob spent the summer in Wiffle-ball games and Sunday night home parties. He even learned to crochet in a special summer course an elderly church member taught for interested group members. Later, Rob realized his informal summer probably had as much impact on the kids as any carefully manicured program would have had.

The Small Church Rewards Generalists

In a small church, no one has just one job. The organist on Sunday morning may also be the church secretary during the week. The worship leader may also coach the church softball team. The head of the women's group may also teach a children's Sunday school class.

In larger churches, however, people specialize. A Sunday school teacher probably won't work with the youth program, and the music leader likely won't prepare communion. People often choose one area of service and stick with it.

Because people are generalists in the small church, a whole set of problems and possibilities arise. Among the problems:

● People get overcommitted. They're committed to the church, so they do whatever they're asked. They either burn themselves out or don't do any of their jobs well.

● People never develop specialized skills. If Clarise leads the youth group, serves on the education committee, sings in the choir, coordinates a women's group and teaches Sunday school, how will she ever develop skills in any single area?

Yet having a church full of generalists also brings possibilities:

● People are flexible. You don't have to rely on a handful of people for the youth ministry. Other church members are willing to learn. After all, they may have tried everything else in the church!

● People know what's going on in the whole church. In larger churches, youth ministry sometimes becomes isolated from other church programs. But when leaders are involved in other areas of church life as well, they know about potential schedule conflicts. They also can think of ways to link youth ministry to other church efforts.

In one small church, the missions committee promoted a community walk for the hungry. One committee member happened also to be a youth leader. So the youth leadership team decided to make the hunger walk a special youth group activity too. Because the leader was a generalist, both the church and the youth program benefited.

● People can use their gifts and talents. Roger always feels pigeonholed in large churches. As soon as they find out he works in public relations, they ask him to join the church's publicity committee.

But Roger has other gifts to share too. He loves music. He has a real commitment to outreach. And he'd like to try his hand at teaching. So when Roger moved to a new city, he and his wife chose a small church. Now he's active on the outreach committee. He still does all the church's publicity in the community. But he also sings in the choir—sometimes even solos. And he teaches the senior high Sunday school class. The kids seem to enjoy it, and he feels he has a real knack for teaching.

The Small Church Is Intergenerational

Compare items from the calendars of small churches vs. large churches:

Small Churches	Large Churches
All-church picnic	Young adult picnic
All-church ice cream social	Youth group ice cream party
Family retreat	Men's retreat
Softball game—everyone come!	Singles' softball game
All-church potluck	Senior citizens' potluck

In small churches, events tend to include all generations. Large churches tend to be segmented by age. Of course, small churches also divide into age groups, and large churches have all-church events. But the balance is different. As Burt writes, "Whether it is by chance, choice, or necessity, the small church's calendar is dominated by events involving children, parents, grandparents, and sometimes great-grandparents (or unrelated people who fill the various roles)."[5]

This tendency has obvious, direct effects on youth ministry in small churches:

• Young people are more actively involved in church life. In large churches, a teenager can be active in the youth group but be unknown in the church as a whole. That won't happen in small churches. Being active in the youth group inevitably means being active in the church, because the young people are included in all-church activities.

• You have fewer opportunities to address specific teenage concerns. One church planned a Valentine's party just for the youth group. But as often happens in small churches, other people wanted to be included—first some college kids; then young adults; then children. By February 14, virtually the whole church was invited. While everyone had a great time (they're used to being together), the leaders weren't able to focus on the teenagers' needs and relationships as they had hoped.

The Small Church Has a Place for Everyone

I'll never forget the time I heard a young deaf girl sing the special music for a small congregation in Iowa. Even though she was painfully off-key, the girl sang her song for the Lord. There wasn't a dry eye in the congregation.

In a larger church with several deaf people, this young woman might have participated only in activities for the hearing impaired. But in this small Iowa church, she was part of the congregation. She sang with and to them. She participated in all church activities. She was a part of the church.

Small churches have room for kids that other groups

reject. While a teenager might be lost in a large youth group, he or she becomes a vital member of a three- or four-member group in a small church. And because small churches tend to care more about people than programs, that young person may be given leadership in the youth group—even in the whole church.

The Small Church Follows a Different Calendar

Churches are like trains: An engine hauling just a few cars will pick up speed much faster than an engine pulling a hundred. The larger the church, the longer it takes to get anything moving. Large churches spend months planning things that a small church could pull together in a few weeks.

Two dynamics account for this. First, it's easier to plan for 10 kids than 100. Suppose a 100-member youth group wants to take a canoe trip. That takes lots of planning—making reservations, gathering deposits, buying food, securing transportation, finding enough chaperones, preparing publicity and on and on. It would take months.

But if a 10-member group wants to take the same trip, details could be worked out in weeks or days. It wouldn't take long to reserve motel rooms and canoes. Food and volunteers would hardly be a problem. Publicity could be reduced to one poster and several telephone calls.

The second dynamic involves church bureaucracy. By necessity, large churches form committees to run programs. Often the structure is formalized with specific lines of authority.

Compare that formal structure to the informal dynamics of small churches. A small church may have just one committee that approves programs. There are fewer channels to follow, approvals to receive and calendars to check. In short, the more flexible structure in many small churches takes the red tape out of the planning process.

While these dynamics make planning quicker and easier, they also can lead to sloppiness. The biggest mistake small church youth leaders make is to stop planning. They become so used to throwing events together that they miss the benefits of carefully planned meetings and events.

The Differences Shape the Ministry

When a small church tries to mimic a large church program, it usually fails. Why? Not because the leaders didn't follow the plans well or because they weren't good leaders. The effort generally fails because the leaders are using the wrong blueprint. They need to develop a program that builds on the strengths of a small church.

This book is filled with ideas that address the unique concerns of small church youth ministries. The next chapter suggests a step-by-step plan for building your customized small church youth ministry.

Endnotes

[1]Lyle Schaller, *The Small Church Is Different!* (Nashville, TN: Abingdon Press, 1982), 12-13.

[2]Schaller, *The Small Church Is Different!*, 27-41.

[3]Gunnar Hoglund, "In Defense of Small Churches," Eternity (May 1984), 35.

[4]Steve Burt, *Activating Leadership in the Small Church* (Valley Forge, PA: Judson Press, 1988), 24.

[5]Burt, *Activating Leadership in the Small Church*, 21.

CHAPTER 3

Building Your Youth Ministry

B uilding a youth program is much like building a house; you do both one brick at a time.

First, builders must decide what to build. What will it look like? Who will live there? What resources are available? When they've decided what to build, they begin by creating a foundation to support the structure. Then they gradually add each part—first the basement; then the floor and walls; finally the roof.

Creating the beauty and comfort of a finished home takes lots of hard work and planning. A solid foundation and sturdy construction keep the house from toppling in a windstorm.

Developing a small church youth ministry requires the same careful planning. For the program to be strong and effective, you must begin with a vision. Then you lay a solid foundation on which to build your structure.

This chapter looks at building a youth ministry in a small church. We'll begin by looking at the plan—what you dream for your ministry. Then we'll examine four building blocks that make a solid foundation. Finally, we'll discuss questions that arise as you build the walls and roof.

A Vision for Ministry

What is your dream for your youth ministry?

That can be a tough question. Some people dream of youth meetings stacked wall to wall with kids. Others dream of mission trips to Chile. Still others dream of a "perfect" youth group—the one with the future Christian celebrity, music star and author in it.

The problem with such dreams is they're generally unrealistic. Most small churches can't afford mission trips to Chile. And the notion of wall-to-wall kids may be completely unrealistic for the community.

What a small church youth ministry needs, then, is a realistic vision of the present and a planned vision for the future.

A vision of the present—Why does your church have a youth ministry? If your only answer is "because we've always had one," then it's time to re-evaluate. Unless you know what you're trying to do, you'll probably never accomplish it.

What are your priorities in youth ministry? Is the youth program primarily an alternative to secular activities? Is it intended to be a close Christian support group for teenagers? Is your priority to minister to kids who are already in the church or to reach out to unchurched teenagers? Is your focus on Bible study or on current issues—or some of both? Small churches can't do everything for all kids. Each of these priorities will shape your youth program.

An excellent way to discover your vision for youth ministry is to develop a mission statement. This statement—which is generally no longer than one or two sentences—captures the essence of what you want to do in youth ministry.

Here's an example: "Broad Street Church's youth ministry seeks to build Christian commitment in teenagers by providing a friendly and open atmosphere for young people to study scripture, develop Christian friendships, serve others in Christ's name and apply their faith to their daily lives."

Include adult youth leaders, teenagers, parents, church staff and interested church members in developing the statement. Once you've agreed on a particular statement, post the statement in your youth room as a reminder. Use it in your planning meetings to help set priorities. And evaluate potential programs by asking yourself, "Do they help us fulfill the priorities we established in our mission statement?"

A vision for the future—In addition to understanding your purpose, you need goals and objectives that build on your mission statement and your dreams. Maybe your vision does include a mission trip to Chile (because you can raise the money). Or maybe it does mean creating a program that attracts lots of kids. But a vision must be realistic for your particular congregation.

Unfortunately, too many small churches try to mimic successful youth programs in large churches. They dream visions with large-church dimensions. They try to build a two-bedroom house with the floor plan of a Hollywood mansion. It just doesn't work.

The secret to a vision for a small church is to build your program using a blueprint that fits your specific needs. Such a blueprint takes into account several factors:

● The dynamics of your community—For example, if you live in a rural town of 800 with seven churches and three youth programs, you'll have trouble realizing a vision of 100 kids in your program. It could happen, but don't count on it.

● The kids' needs—Remember your ministry will have little impact if it doesn't meet kids' needs. A church might envision, for example, a Friday night fellowship following high school ball games. It may be a neat idea on paper. And it may have funding and even adult support. But if the kids already participate in healthy after-game activities, the program probably won't work. Why? Because it doesn't take into account kids' needs.

There are dozens of ways to discover kids' needs. Attend a student council meeting at a high school. Survey kids using a tool such as *Determining Needs in Your Youth Ministry*.[1] Talk individually with group members about what they need from the church. Throw an overnight dream party with pizza, games and videos—and spend the night listening to kids' ideas. Talk to parents about their concerns. Whatever methods you use, find out what kids need before developing programs.

● The church's style—Youth ministry in a small church isn't isolated from the congregation. As we learned in Chapter 2, small churches are characterized by intergenerational activities and emphases.

It's important, then, to build on the church's strengths rather than trying to make the youth ministry completely distinct from the church. If your congregation has had a long-time emphasis on missions and service, your youth program can have a parallel emphasis. If your church has a strong tradition of Bible study and discipleship, those same emphases can carry over into your youth ministry. Or if your church is known as a friendly place, the same attributes will likely show in your youth program. Both the church and the youth ministry will be stronger as you augment the church's character and style in your youth ministry.

● Realistic intermediate objectives—If your dream is to attract 20 new kids to the youth program this year, what objectives could you have to reach those kids? How will you attain the goals? What resources will you need? How much will it cost? Where will you hold meetings when you've grown that much?

It's one thing to dream about adding 20 new kids. It's another to actually make that vision come true. Use the "Reaching the Vision" worksheet with your youth ministry team to set goals and intermediate objectives. By planning intermediate objectives for reaching your goals, you multiply your chances of success.

Key Building Blocks

Once you know what you want to accomplish through your youth ministry, it's time to lay your foundation. Here are four building blocks to ensure your ministry's effectiveness. Together, the blocks spell L-I-F-E.

Love—I once paraphrased 1 Corinthians 13 for youth workers. It goes like this:

Reaching the Vision

1. Brainstorm and agree on your youth ministry team's dreams for the next five years. Write your dreams down. Limit yourself to two or three major dreams per year.

   a. In one year:

   b. In two years:

   c. In three years:

   d. In four years:

   e. In five years:

2. Now analyze each dream for the first year using these questions:

   a. What costs are involved? (Be as specific as possible.)

   b. What adult help is needed?

   c. Do you need any special permission to pursue this goal? If so, what must you do to get it?

   d. What kids have special abilities to help fulfill this dream?

3. Set several objectives for each first-year goal. For example, if your goal is to create a youth room, some objectives might be to get permission from the church board, clean out the room and hold a fund-raiser for new equipment. Think of all the objectives to complete the job. Assign each objective a date for completion and a person responsible.

4. Check progress through the year to be sure people are fulfilling responsibilities to make dreams become realities.

Though I lead creative meetings using all the latest methods, but do so without love, my teaching is as noisy rush-hour traffic or as clawing of fingernails on a chalkboard.

If I know all the latest trends in youth ministry, and understand all the mysteries of why young people actually like heavy metal music and superficial teenage magazines, and if I own every book, video and youth worker magazine, but don't love, I'm useless to kids.

True love is patient when eighth graders chatter during my Sunday night series on Jeremiah. It's kind when they tease me about my rapidly receding hairline and my equally increasing midline. Love doesn't envy young people when they can still spike a volleyball—and I can hardly jump to the occasion. It doesn't boast about my past success with "better" youth groups.

Love doesn't cut down. It doesn't say "I told you so" when a kid who has eaten nothing but chocolate shakes and fries on a youth trip gets sick in the back of the church van.

Love for teenagers overcomes all frustrations, professes all truth, delivers all hope and suffers all trouble.

Such love will never die. Where there are programs, they will become outdated. Where there are teaching abilities, they will eventually lose their edge. Where there is understanding of youth culture, it will vanish as times change.

Programs, abilities and love are all important to youth work. But the greatest of these is love.

I believe sincere love and care for young people is the cornerstone in a youth program. Love is particularly vital in small churches that focus their ministries on building one-to-one relationships.

If the leaders don't love kids, the program will never be

effective. In contrast, if leaders love kids, their love can overcome numerous barriers.

Simply put, anybody can be an effective and successful
youth worker. But the ministry must flow from a love for
today's young people. Kids don't care how much you know
until they know how much you care.

Therefore, laying the first brick in your youth ministry
structure involves finding adult leaders who sincerely love kids.
There's no age limit. I've seen 50- and 60-year olds who've
done a great job. It all depends on the person.

Chapter 6 focuses on finding youth ministry volunteers.
This process isn't as hard as it may seem. Simply stop and
listen. Which adults in the church talk with kids? Which adults
do kids hang around?

Barbara was having trouble getting youth workers for the
high school group. She had advertised and begged for volunteers. But no one expressed interest. Then one Sunday after
church, Barbara noticed Harry "shadow-boxing" with Bill, a
high schooler. Barbara watched the two roughhouse for several
minutes before they noticed her.

"Hey, Harry, you're not bad," Barbara joked, "that kind of
sparring would win you a gold medal in our annual youth
group pillow fight!"

"Well, I don't know about that," Harry responded, trying
hard to catch his breath. "Bill's tough!"

Two weeks later, Barbara found Harry in a local coffee
shop with Tom and Rick, two youth group members. He was
taking them fishing that afternoon.

It clicked. Harry had youth ministry potential.

"Hey, Harry, would you be interested in working with the
youth group?" Barbara asked the next Sunday.

"I dunno. Been quite a while," Harry replied. "I'm not
much of a teacher. That's why I quit. Our old youth minister
thought it would be best—said I was out of touch."

"You don't look out of touch to me," Barbara shot back.
"Want to give it another try?"

"Well, I . . . uh . . ."

"C'mon Harry!" Rick exclaimed, walking up behind Harry

to give him a bear hug. "It'd be great. We'd have a blast!"

"Besides, you won't have to teach if you don't want to," Barbara interjected. "We just need the extra help."

"Let me think about it," Harry offered.

The next week, Harry accepted the job. Several years later, he still works with kids in that small Illinois church. No, he doesn't get rave reviews when he leads meetings. And he's not much on all the games.

But he does love the kids—even though he's 84.

Involvement—A lot of people say, "Young people are the church of tomorrow." There's some truth to that. But young people are the church of *today* as well. So instead of waiting for them to grow up, we're called to help them become active parts of the church today. Only then will they mature into church leaders for tomorrow.

Chapter 1 listed opportunities for involvement as a key benefit of small churches. Youth groups in larger churches sometimes become separated from the rest of the church because they have their own programs for everything. But in a small church, young people can participate in numerous all-church activities.

Small churches that discover creative ways to include teen-agers in the church see young people blossom in leadership skills and Christian commitment. Many churches have kids lead youth services, usher for church or lead in worship. But there are dozens of creative ways to get kids involved.

How about encouraging kids to be "preacher for a day" or "youth minister for a day" or "church secretary for a day"? During school breaks, have young people sign up for different church staff positions. Then have them each learn from the staff person they selected by spending a typical day together. Such an experience gives young people an inside look at the church and its ministry. And it might even nudge a young person to consider full-time Christian service as a career. Chapter 5 gives lots more ideas for developing leadership in teenagers.

Fellowship—Another vital building block of a small church youth program is fellowship. Kids want to be accepted and loved by adults and peers. Because of the intimacy that's possible in small churches, a youth program can provide that acceptance.

Fellowship and social activities aren't frivolous time-killers. They provide opportunities for young people to develop close Christian friendships. In the process, young people will learn to love and accept each other.

Christian fellowship is more than a clique of good friends. Christian fellowship is accepting each other as brothers and sisters because "there is neither Jew nor Greek, slave nor free, male nor female, for you are all one in Christ Jesus" (Galatians 3:28). It means accepting and loving other people—even though they're different.

Many small church youth groups have problems with cliques—particularly if the kids have known each other since their first diapers. These cliques can be major stumbling blocks to unity and acceptance. Newcomers are automatically outsiders, and breaking into the circle can take months—or even years.

Carolyne was new in town. On her first Sunday at a small church, she hung close to her mom. They'd been visiting several churches, looking for a church home. Up to now, they'd had little luck. Every church seemed alike—cold and unfriendly.

The last church they visited left Carolyne in tears. She'd really hoped to find a friend—just one—at Sunday school. But when she walked in and sat down, the other kids laughed and joked among themselves, telling about their Friday night adventures.

No one spoke to Carolyne.

Sunday school dragged on eternally before Carolyne finally could reunite with her mom for worship. But the service wasn't much different. Even after the pastor introduced Carolyne's family to the church, few greeted the two. And no young person said a word.

Now, a week later, Carolyne was beginning to hate her new town. As she walked across the church parking lot, she braced herself for another awful Sunday morning.

"Hi, how ya doing?"

Carolyne turned with a jump when she heard the cheerful voice behind her.

"I'm Shari. What's your name?"

"Uh . . . Carolyne," she answered, still stunned.

"I'm heading to Sunday school," Shari continued. "Hope you'll join us."

Carolyne did, and the difference was unbelievable. Before she left church that day, she had an invitation to go out for pizza with youth group members. After just one Sunday, Carolyne felt this church could be her home.

Carolyne was accepted even though she wasn't really attractive and her clothes weren't the greatest. She was accepted because of who she was.

That acceptance was particularly important for Carolyne. She's blind. She needs friends she can trust. And she finally found them—even though she was different.

Christian fellowship may not come naturally for kids at first. But you can improve it in numerous ways:

● Measure your group's level of acceptance by having group members complete the "Do Others Feel Welcome?" worksheet. Total all the kids' responses to each question to show which areas are best in your group (the highest combined scores) and which areas need improvement (the lowest combined scores).

Brainstorm ways to improve in the weaker areas. Have kids think of what could make the group more accepting. Then give the group the same survey six months later to measure improvements.

● Use group-building activities in your meetings. Denny Rydberg's book *Building Community in Youth Groups* (Group Books) gives dozens of ideas.

● Encourage outgoing kids to welcome people to your meetings.

● Have times for one-to-one sharing during your meetings. Have partners ask each other about their families and backgrounds.

Education—Many small church youth programs focus so

Do Others Feel Welcome?

Instructions: Circle the number that best represents your attitudes and action:

	Right on Target			Wishful Thinking	
1. If someone I don't know walks into the church, I'll make a special effort to get acquainted.	5	4	3	2	1
2. I'm always ready for our youth group to grow—even though a newcomer might change my friendship with other group members.	5	4	3	2	1
3. I like the people we have in our group right now, but I'm always ready to become a good friend to a newcomer.	5	4	3	2	1
4. I know everyone in our youth group fairly well.	5	4	3	2	1
5. Our group would welcome anyone to our fellowship.	5	4	3	2	1
6. I'm an easy person to get to know.	5	4	3	2	1
7. I'm good at welcoming and accepting newcomers into our group.	5	4	3	2	1

Now score yourself:
●If most of your answers are fours or fives, great! Your group is accepting and open to newcomers and has potential for growth.
●If most of your answers are ones, twos or threes, think of why it's wishful thinking to expect newcomers to feel accepted in your group. On paper, list actions or attitudes that would move your answers to fours or fives. Then for starters, choose one action or attitude to work on to improve your "acceptance ability."

much energy on entertaining that they fail to educate. While there's nothing wrong with having fun, it isn't an adequate basis for youth ministry.

I used to be Mr. Fun N. Games. My youth group meetings were often little more than crazy crowdbreakers and silly skits. We always did off-the-wall activities. And the kids ate up the meetings like they were ice cream sundaes.

Of course, about halfway through each meeting, we'd stop for a short (often poorly prepared) lesson. But the lesson was a token gesture, not a vital part of the meeting.

The youth group experienced some problems and kids started leaving like geese in autumn. I couldn't understand—especially when some former members joined another church across town.

Then it hit me one evening while eating dinner. Spread out before me was everything from chocolate cake to carrots. My first inclination was to grab the tasty sweets. But eating dessert first ruins the meal. Plus dessert doesn't have much nutritional value. Chocolate cake is great, but carrots are far more important.

The analogy fit my youth group.

My chocolate cake programming was popular with that hungry bunch of kids. But such a high-calorie emphasis wasn't spiritually nutritious. In time, the kids either starved from spiritual malnutrition or left for a better meal elsewhere.

The secret is to provide a spiritually balanced meal. We can learn creative meeting recipes that will be both tasty and nutritious.

The best recipe for a tasty and spiritually balanced meal uses the ingredients of active learning. This technique gets kids involved so they actually experience what you want them to learn. In their book *Do It! Active Learning in Youth Ministry*, Thom and Joani Schultz write:

> The need for active learning in youth ministry is greater today than in generations past. Today's media-wise teenagers get bored easily. They've grown up in an unprecedented kaleidoscope of

media images, concert extravaganzas, video games, computer wizardry and a high-tech explosion of information. Our longstanding approaches to Christian education don't stand a chance in our teenagers' fast-paced world.[2]

The Schultzes suggest seven characteristics of active learning:

• Active learning is an adventure. You can't always predict what will happen, but the surprises are usually great opportunities for learning.

• Active learning is fun and/or captivating. It intrigues kids. Because they're interested, they learn more.

• Active learning involves everyone. If everyone gets involved in the learning experience, everyone learns.

• Active learning is student-based, not teacher-based. Through active learning, students discover truth instead of passively waiting for teachers to impart facts and ideas.

• Active learning is process-oriented. Students learn as much from the learning process as they learn from the specific information shared.

• Active learning is focused through debriefing. By talking about the learning experience afterward, students sort through the information and feelings and apply them to their lives.

• Active learning is relational. Because everyone's involved, students interact with each other and reveal bits of themselves. In the process, their relationships grow.[3]

Once you start looking, you'll discover dozens of ways to involve kids in learning. Hold kids "hostage" in a dark closet and share stories of persecution and martyrdom. Learn servanthood by washing one another's feet. Having a meeting about death? Tour a local mortuary or walk through an old graveyard. Dealing with Jesus walking on water? Secure a boat and hold the meeting in the middle of a lake. (You may even challenge a few to try walking on the water!) A lesson on feeding the poor can come alive when kids work in a soup kitchen or local food bank.

The resource list on page 164 includes several valuable resources for active learning. By using this approach, your kids will learn to enjoy the healthy main courses as well as the desserts in your youth ministry.

Some Building Techniques

"Congratulations! You're our new youth group sponsor."

Kim sighed with nervous relief as she hung up the phone. She had worked with the youth group a couple of years, but had never been in charge of the program. Even though Kim admitted she had never done some of the things in her job description, the pastor still felt confident she could do the work.

But Kim wasn't so sure. She had so many questions about how to build a small church program. How many activities can I do? What about small classes? Do I combine the junior and senior high?

Let's look at some questions about building a small church youth program.

How much programming is appropriate? Large church youth ministries always have something going on—youth group meetings, Bible studies, service projects, choir, Sunday school, support groups and on and on. Kids pick and choose what they want to do, and different people are responsible for the different ministries.

Such an extensive program is unrealistic and inappropriate in small churches. It's important to gear your program to your kids and your specific situation. Some churches may need just a weekly meeting to keep kids active and growing. Others may want a variety of options to meet different needs, expecting only a few kids to attend each program. Flexibility is the key.

Consider these options—but don't feel limited by them:

• Program one youth meeting (games, community-builders and topical studies) and one Bible study each week. Then, once a month, do an outside activity such as going to a movie, heading for the beach or visiting a museum.

• Meet informally. For example, go watch the high school

basketball game every Friday night, then head for a fast-food restaurant or pizza place for a "fifth quarter" Bible study or fellowship time.

• Have one regular meeting each week, but vary the format from week to week. For example, do Bible study one week, group-building the next, outreach the next, and a topical study the final week of the month. If a month has a fifth meeting day, plan a special event.

If most kids don't come, should we cancel the program? In his book, *Great Ideas for Small Youth Groups,* Wayne Rice tells about planning a camping trip for the youth group. As the date approached, he discovered most kids wouldn't be able to go. In fact, three days before the trip, only three kids had signed up.

"My first inclination," Rice writes, "was to reschedule the trip for a better weekend when most of the group could come. My reasoning was undeniably sound—we were still going to have to do the same amount of work and preparation for three kids as twenty—so why not postpone it until later."

But Rice decided not to cancel, because three kids *had* signed up, and they'd be disappointed if the trip was called off. "We went ahead with our plans and climbed the mountain with three kids and our guest speaker. We had a wonderful time . . . Those three kids felt very special, and the two days with them gave me a chance to get to know them and minister to them in a personal way."[4]

This story illustrates an important key to small church youth ministry: Instead of complaining about who *isn't* there, celebrate who *is*. Those kids who come are valuable children of God, and you risk communicating to them they're not worth your time if you cancel meetings and programs.

Instead of canceling the program, enjoy the opportunity to build relationships in the intimacy of a smaller group. Try these ideas:

• Adapt the program to fit the smaller group. Instead of breaking into groups, work on a project together.

• Have optional activities in mind. If you plan a crowdbreaker but only two kids come, switch to another

community-building activity for two people.
  • Change plans completely. If your program simply won't
work with one or two kids, surprise the kids by announcing a
special meeting at the ice cream parlor or pizza place or in
your own living room. Spend the time getting to know the kids
on a deeper level.
  Should we combine junior and senior high? Let's look
at both sides of this question, beginning with advantages of
keeping your junior and senior highers together:
  • A family atmosphere—Keeping groups together can
foster a "big brother/little brother" family atmosphere. Junior
highers look up to older kids, and high schoolers have an
opportunity to be Christlike examples for younger kids.
  I've led youth groups where older students helped
younger kids adjust to the youth group. For example, when a
noisy junior higher would disrupt the meeting, an older group
member would quiet him or her through positive peer pressure
and example.
  • Flexibility—If you keep kids together, you have more
flexibility for programming. For example, playing volleyball
with 10 people is much easier than with four or five. And since
curriculum is often geared for larger groups, having more kids
means you don't have to adapt the materials as much.
  • Continuity in the group—Teenagers need to feel they
belong. One advantage of keeping junior and senior highers
together is that it helps them develop long-term friendships
with kids of different ages.
  Other dynamics suggest dividing the young people by age.
Consider these disadvantages of keeping the group together:
  • Developmental differences—You don't have to be an
expert in adolescent development to see that high school
seniors live in a different world from seventh-graders. A senior
thinks about choosing a college, selecting the right mate and
planning for the future. A seventh-grader thinks about how to
survive fifth-period math, what's going on in his or her
changing body and whether members of the opposite sex are
fun to tease.
  These differences make it difficult to meet the wide range

of needs. It's tough to prepare Bible studies and youth group meetings that appeal to all ages, since most seventh-graders still think concretely and seniors think more abstractly. Thus a topic that's exciting to a junior higher often bores a senior higher—and vice versa.

• Senior highers' attitudes—You'll rarely attract new senior highers to a combined group. Some mature seniors won't tolerate noisy, immature junior highers. To keep them together could hurt—even kill—your group. As more junior highers enter the program, the remaining high schoolers will silently leave.

• Group dynamics—If combining the ages creates a large group, natural group dynamics will actually pre-empt some of the advantages you seek to create. In my experience, youth groups with 20 members must divide to create more growth.

If you choose to have just one group, make provisions for different developmental needs. I've lost kids because I waited too long to form two separate groups. One way to balance the advantages and disadvantages of combining groups is to combine sometimes and form two groups other times. Divide into two groups for Bible and topical studies. Then during activities where both age groups can benefit (such as recreation), let them stay together.

What can we do with just one or two kids? You don't need lots of kids to have a significant youth ministry. In fact, your ministry with one or two kids may have a greater impact than a large program with dozens of kids.

Youth worker Dean Feldmeyer tells about having trouble getting kids to sign up for an inner-city workcamp. When he investigated, he found the youth group guys didn't want to go because they'd miss practice for the cross-country team. So he suggested they have daily workouts at the camp. They agreed to go.

Feldmeyer describes the experience: "Every morning we got up an hour before everyone else and jogged five miles through the inner city. We saw sights no one else in the camp saw. We had an hour of quiet talk without interruption . . . Granted, the guys had to slow down a bit for me to keep up.

But what they sacrificed in training they made up in personal growth. Years later, I still have a special bond with those guys. We remember those mornings whenever we're together."[5]

If you have only two or three kids in your group, don't try to imitate the big church down the street with its multiple programs. Instead, concentrate on building personal relationships with the kids you have. Be a spiritual mentor for them. Challenge them to grow and lead in the church.

What happens when we have a Sunday school class with only one teenager? I experienced this frustration in one church and had a tough time solving it.

We had classes for first- and second-graders, third- and fourth-graders, fifth- and sixth-graders and junior and senior high. Attendance through fourth grade was steady, and the junior and senior high class averaged eight to 10. But sandwiched between was a single sixth-grade girl, with no one in fifth grade.

In the process of deciding what to do, I considered several options:

• Combine several classes into one; then have each young person study the lesson at his or her own age level.

• Promote the lone young person to the next age group, thus eliminating the class until it's needed.

• Use the single student as a teacher's aide for a younger class.

• Let the young person select a topic of his or her choice, research it and present the findings to another class.

I wanted to divide the junior and senior high class and promote the girl to junior high. But the church had never changed its Sunday school classes, and saw no reason to start. So we maintained a Sunday school class for that girl the whole year. She grew through the experience, then joined the junior high group the next year at the traditional time.

What can we do if there's not a good meeting space for the youth group? If you walk into many small churches for Sunday school, you'll find several circles of people sitting around the sanctuary. Each is carrying on its own conversation. Each is a separate Sunday school class.

Space is limited for many churches. They don't have special rooms for each age group or class. And so the youth group may not have a "youth room." Instead, it may share a room with the children and young adults. Or the youth group may get stuck in a musty basement corner.

Other small churches have the opposite problem. They meet in huge, old buildings with large rooms. Teenagers feel lost and intimidated by the space.

Yet appropriate space is an important concern for an effective youth program. Rice writes: "Room dynamics can dramatically affect the spirit and tone of a meeting. When the room feels full, the atmosphere is one of excitement as well as intimacy. But it's difficult to feel intimate when the meeting place is so large that voices echo."[6]

Here are some suggestions to make your space fit your group:

• Don't put out too many chairs. It's better to have to add places to sit than to have too many. When chairs are empty, the group feels even smaller. And it subtly emphasizes who's not there, instead of who is.

• Meet in homes. If you have a small group, a living room can be an ideal setting for youth group meetings. You'll have a comfortable place to meet, and you'll usually have the added benefit of extra programming helps: a kitchen for refreshments, a stereo for music, a television for videos. One word of caution: When you meet in a home, find ways to deal with distractions such as in-and-out traffic, a crying baby, the telephone or pets.

• If you meet in a large room or share a room with another group, set aside part of the room as the youth group space. Use partitions, bookshelves or even sheets of crepe paper to define the space. Decorate the walls with pictures from youth group events and posters. Use carpet samples or pillows on the floor for casual seating. If the room has a high ceiling, you might even make a false ceiling with a sheet.

• Adapt unused space. There may be space in the church that's not being used efficiently. Maybe a room that's been piled up with junk. Or an adjoining building that's not in use.

With a little creativity, you may be able to turn the unused space into a youth room. Rice tells about a California group that transformed an old tool shed behind the church into the youth room. They repaired it to ensure it was safe, painted it, decorated it and dubbed it "The Shack."[7]

How do we deal with siblings in the youth group?
Brothers and sisters are blessings and curses to youth groups. They're blessings when they cooperate and have a strong relationship. They're curses when they bring their family bickering and rivalries to the youth group. As youth worker Scott Linscott writes: "[Siblings] know each other well—maybe too well. They know things about each other that people outside the home don't know. And they're only too glad to pass this privileged information on to people outside the family."[8]

In both cases, they're a fact of small church youth ministry. If a small church has four teenagers, two may be brother and sister—and the other two cousins! Larger churches may have the luxury of putting siblings in different classes, on different teams and in charge of different projects. But not small churches. That's why you need to find ways to accent the positive in their family relationship—and diminish the negative.

A basic principle is to remember that each group member is an individual. Linscott writes: "The cardinal rule is to treat each sibling as an individual and not as a unit of two people who belong to the same group. Larry is Larry and Sue is Sue. Don't think of Larry and Sue together in youth group."[9]

Here are some ideas to keep sibling relationships from becoming a problem in your church:

● Establish guidelines for siblings to follow at church that will keep home life and church life separate. Make sure everyone understands and accepts the principles. It's fun to develop these with the kids—it can be a good activity to address family issues and concerns. Linscott developed the guidelines in the "Ten Commandments for Siblings in Youth Group" box, which gives you some ideas.

● Encourage siblings to share positive memories and experiences with the group. Help them enhance their family rela-

Ten Commandments for
Siblings in Youth Group[10]

 Thou shalt not tell embarrassing stories about thy brothers or sisters in public.

 Thou shalt not analyze thy brother's or sister's problems in the midst of the youth group.

 Thou shalt not run home and tell thy parents of all the "naughties" thy brother or sister hath committed at youth group functions. Thou shalt leave that up to thy youth leader.

 Thou shalt not talk about thy brother's or sister's disgusting personal habits during sharing times.

 Thou shalt not run to thy youth leader and talk of all the "naughties" thy brother or sister hath committed at home. Thou shalt leave that up to thy parents.

 Thou shalt not blab to the youth assembly that thy brother or sister flunketh English.

 Thou shalt not try to discipline thy brother or sister at youth group functions. Thou shalt leave that up to thy youth leader.

 Thou shalt not beat upon thy brother or sister at youth group. Thou shalt wait until later.

 Thou shalt respect thy brother's or sister's property at all times.

 Thou shalt have a blast and be well-loved by thy youth leaders if thou wilt honor these commandments.

Reprinted by permission from GROUP Magazine, copyright © 1987, Thom Schultz Publications, Inc., Box 481, Loveland, CO 80539.

tionship through the youth group.

• When possible, put siblings on different teams or projects or in different discussion groups.

• Instead of joint mail, send mail to each sibling. And don't tell one sibling information that's meant for the other.

• If siblings become a problem in the youth group, talk with them about it privately. Help them deal with their differences and come up with specific ways they can work to make their relationship more healthy.

How can we have a youth group if we don't have any kids? Starting a youth group from scratch is never easy. It's hard to attract kids to a church where there are no other kids. If you're in this situation, try one of these options:

• Check to see if any church families have teenagers who aren't active in the church. Kids may have dropped out because nothing was offered that appealed to them. Visit with these kids and find out what would interest them. Then plan events to respond to their interests. These kids could form your youth group core.

• Work with adults in the church to plan a high-profile event to attract kids to your church. Widely publicize the event and try to build community interest. Through the event, try to discover kids who aren't involved—but are interested—in a youth program. Then build from there.

• Go where the kids are. The mall. Schools. Ball games. Consider substitute teaching or coaching in your local school system (if it's permitted), or offer to sponsor special events or programs for students.

Once you've established contact with kids, start meeting their needs. Suggest that several of them join you on a trip to the beach. Round up kids to play weekly basketball games, or offer counseling or support groups to kids with specific needs.

One youth worker in Florida worked closely with his local school system by chaperoning school dances, volunteering as a school counselor and serving as an assistant coach for the football team. Through such contacts, the youth worker—who developed the principal's trust—was able to form an alternative support group for teenagers during study hall.

At first the support group dealt with issues such as peer pressure, alcohol abuse and adolescent sexuality. In time, however, the group focused more on personal needs such as self-image, problems with parents and the need to belong.

Eventually, the group moved out of the school and into the youth worker's church for a Bible study. Today the group continues to grow and meet the needs of high school kids.

The Master Builder

Putting all these pieces together may seem difficult. Can people in small churches really do it?

If you try to do it alone, you can't. But with God's help, all things are possible.

Psalm 127:1 says, "Unless the Lord builds the house, its builders labor in vain." Regardless of your dreams, efforts, sweat, programs and expertise, you're not really the builder. God is.

That's why your youth ministry planning and leadership should be bathed with prayer. Seek God's guidance in planning. Evoke God's leadership in each meeting, Bible study and special event.

With God's help, your youth ministry will become a house of God where young people feel at home.

Endnotes

[1] Peter L. Benson and Dorothy L. Williams, *Determining Needs in Your Youth Ministry* (Loveland, CO: Group Books, 1987).

[2] Thom and Joani Schultz, *Do It! Active Learning in Youth Ministry* (Loveland, CO: Group Books, 1989), 29-30.

[3] Schultz and Schultz, *Do It! Active Learning in Youth Ministry*, 10-15.

[4] Wayne Rice, *Great Ideas for Small Youth Groups* (Grand Rapids, MI: Zondervan Publishing House, 1986), 39-40.

[5] Dean Feldmeyer, "When Less Than 2 or 3 Are Gathered," GROUP Magazine (June-August 1988), 63.

[6] Rice, *Great Ideas for Small Youth Groups*, 40.

[7] Rice, *Great Ideas for Small Youth Groups*, 41.

[8] Scott Linscott, "When Siblings Squabble in Your Group," GROUP Magazine (September 1987), 28.

[9] Linscott, "When Siblings Squabble in Your Group," 29.

[10] Linscott, "When Siblings Squabble in Your Group," 28.

CHAPTER 4

Creating a Healthy Youth Ministry

I f only there was a magic potion or a step-by-step plan for creating a successful small church youth ministry. But there's not. And there can't be. Just as a doctor must prescribe medication for a specific ailment, every small church has to respond to its particular kids' needs.

At the same time, doctors agree that exercising, maintaining a balanced diet and staying away from certain high-risk behaviors can contribute to a healthier body for anyone. Similarly, there are some common elements that foster a healthy youth ministry.

Successful small church youth ministry is balanced. It includes Bible studies and games—and everything in between. It has something for all teenagers. It reaches out to the non-Christian. It remembers the lukewarm Christian who's struggling with difficult questions. And it stretches the committed young person toward even deeper faith and commitment.

This chapter lists several elements of a strong and healthy youth program. These elements are often the keys to group growth. However, this list is not a prescription. Each individual program must weigh each element according to the youth ministry's goals and purposes.

And the list doesn't have a money-back guarantee. Following all the guidelines and suggestions for maintaining good health doesn't guarantee that you'll never be sick. Elements beyond your control ultimately determine your health.

Small church youth ministry works the same way.

One-to-One Relationships

Small church youth ministry begins and ends with relationships. Adult leaders must relate well to kids. And programming should be designed to help kids develop relationships among themselves.

Enhancing adult-teenager relationships—Some adults who don't naturally get along with teenagers think the generation gap is unbridgeable. So they maintain their distance from teenagers and never build relationships with them.

However, to be effective in ministry, youth leaders need to build relationships with teenagers. That's easier if you work with a smaller group of kids. Here are some tips to get started:

• Go where kids are. Stop for a moment and think where you see kids the most. The local mall. School. Friday night football games. It's easier to build relationships on their turf than on yours.

Don't expect instant results. Relationship-building requires trust—and trust takes time. But you have to make the first move.

• Become a student of youth culture. Take time to watch the TV shows kids watch. Listen to kids' music. Read a teenage magazine.

Perhaps the biggest mistake adults make in building relationships with kids involves lack of understanding *current* youth culture. Ask yourself the following questions:

1. What's a current Top 10 song, performer or video?
2. What's one of the hottest teenage fashions?
3. Which current movie has kids talking?
4. What are three TV shows kids watch these days?

As these questions indicate, being a student of youth culture is continuous. Every day, something new is "hot." A successful pop song will hit the Top 10 for only a few weeks. This year's teenage idol may be the brunt of jokes next year.

You don't have to buy anything to know what's hot. Just look and listen. Kids will tell you what's in—through their speech, clothing and actions.

• Be yourself. While it's important to be in touch with kids' culture, it's just as important to be an adult. It's good to know what kids are wearing, saying and watching, but kids can see through any superficial attempts to be like them. They're not looking for a hair style or a rock concert companion in a youth worker. Rather, they need an adult who cares and understands.

• Take risks in relationships. This may mean failure. It may mean a kid will turn against you. But as Jesus said, "Greater love has no one than this, that he lay down his life for his friends" (John 15:13). Loving kids will never be easy. Just when you think they're coming around, you may find them heading the other way. A risk can change a kid forever. But if you never risk, you'll never know.

Fostering relationships among teenagers—Teenagers will get involved in their youth group if they feel close to other group members. Thus it's important to help group members develop healthy relationships with each other.

Often friendships develop naturally in small groups as kids share experiences, needs and concerns with each other. But you can also promote good relationships in many different ways:

• Use group-building activities during your meetings— even if it's the same four kids who show up each week. Always assume kids don't know everything about each other. Have fun learning about people's interests, backgrounds, pet peeves and favorite foods.

• Have regular sharing times when teenagers express their views and concerns. People draw closer when they understand each other.

• Emphasize gifts such as hospitality and a listening ear. Challenge your kids to develop a closer awareness of each other.

• Have kids work on projects together, such as collecting food for the hungry or toys for low-income children. Too many youth groups spend time competing among themselves. Instead, pull the group together through shared activities.

Need-Oriented Programming

What topics should youth groups focus on?

"Drugs, sex and rock 'n' roll!" a youth worker in Illinois quickly responded when I asked that question.

Why are they the problems?

"I can't tell you," he responded. "But they're the reason our program is falling apart."

After talking more I learned the real reason his kids were into "the big three"—poor self-image.

Most of his young people were starving for someone to say they amounted to something. When they couldn't get affirmation at home or church, they turned to heavy metal music, necking and crack. The youth leader became so concerned about the outward problems that he missed the real needs.

Too often, youth programs attack kids without understanding them or meeting their needs. Or programs focus on esoteric topics ("The Monastic Movement of the Inter-Testamental Period") that don't interest the kids. So they don't come.

Sometimes leaders assume they know all the needs because they know the kids well. But that's not always true—even in a small group.

Discover needs by talking to kids about their concerns. Find out what's bothering them, what they're struggling with, and what they have questions about. Then address those concerns in a Christian context.

J.T. serves a small church in Seattle. He had few "big" problems until the day a youth group member committed suicide. The young man was a school leader and a top student. His death—two days before graduation—triggered a rash of suicides. Within a week, four more kids were dead. Two were from J.T.'s youth group.

With each hour possibly holding another suicide attempt,

J.T. called the youth group together. Because of his strong relationship with the small group, he addressed the issue with a candid message. He shared how he almost took his life, and how God has spared him and his family the tragedy. He spoke of life's purpose. He shared his own weaknesses.

The hours that followed revealed a stunning peer pressure to commit suicide, largely stemming from a current movie. J.T. and his group talked about their friends' deaths. His group members shared deep feelings of how they thought about committing suicide as well. They related the movie's story line and even acknowledged popular songs and books that glorified suicide as an answer to life's problems.

By the end of the meeting, the young people committed themselves to life—not death. They agreed to support and encourage one another through this difficult time.

It must have worked. The string of suicides was over.

Another way to discover needs is to have kids complete surveys in which you ask about their needs, worries and interests. I conducted an extensive survey with my suburban youth group and discovered a poor self-image was the real problem underlying the materialism I saw in the group. When I started addressing the disease instead of the symptom, I made real progress.

As you uncover needs, remember different kids have different needs—even if you just have two or three kids. New Christians may be ready only for developing Christian friendships and learning what it means to be a Christian. Other teenagers might be ready for deeper discussions about faith and Christian commitment.

It's important, then, to provide a balance. And you can know the appropriate balance only when you know your kids.

Family Support and Ministry

Chapter 2 explained that small churches tend to be intergenerational. While it's important for every age group to have individual activities, a small church youth program will be much more successful if it includes regular opportunities for families to do things together.

There are dozens of activities families can do together. Plan special youth meetings that include parents. Several meetings are included in *Ministry to Families With Teenagers* by Dub Ambrose and Walt Mueller.[1] Allow parents and teenagers to interact. Plan social activities too. Offer family nights at a local YMCA or school gym. Organize fun nights for fellowship. Take trips, as a church family, to local attractions.

You can also help families through parent education and support. Offer parenting seminars. Have youth group members sponsor free babysitting so parents can have a night out. Collect research on family issues and publish a monthly parent newsletter. Or order a bulk subscription to a parents newsletter such as PARENTS & TEENAGERS.[2]

Finally, don't forget to pray for parents. Maybe even send a note of encouragement from time to time.

Spiritual Growth and Discipleship

The element most often overlooked in a small church youth group is spiritual growth or discipleship. Youth leaders sometimes find it easier just to have fun activities. Often they're so worried about scaring kids away that they don't push them spiritually. Or they don't want to take the necessary time to disciple young people.

Many young people are eager to grow spiritually. They tire of superficial meetings and games. They want to discover how to apply their faith to their lives.

The small church can be an ideal setting for discipleship training, since the best discipleship programs are one-to-one. Through a personal relationship with a mentor, a young person can learn what it means to be a mature Christian.

One youth minister began by focusing on helping one teenager grow spiritually. They prayed together, studied the Bible together and shared questions and insights about their Christian walk.

The next year, the leader chose a different teenager to mentor. And the first teenager became a mentor for a peer.

One plus one. Two plus two. Four plus four. In time, the whole group was involved in mentoring.

Of course, developing a trusting relationship means exposing your weaknesses and faults. That's not easy. But in the process of discipling teenagers, we are drawn to new spiritual depths as well.

Friendship Evangelism

Part of our calling as Christians is to reach other people for Christ. Christ gave the church the job of reaching the world (Matthew 28:18-20). And teenagers can participate in that Great Commission.

When they hear the word "evangelism," many young people think of standing on a street corner handing out tracts. But effective evangelism involves building relationships and— as trust builds—sharing the gospel story and how God has touched their lives. In his book *Friends and Faith*, Larry Keefauver writes that 70 to 90 percent of Christians come to Christ because of a friend's invitation. Less than 1 percent become Christians through crusades.[3]

It's exciting to see kids sharing their faith with friends. But it takes time to bring kids to that point. Here are some steps to get you started:

• **Emphasize outreach in your program.** Remind kids—even though they seem small in number—they have a mission to reach their friends for Christ. Use films, topical studies, suggested readings and lessons.

• **Teach kids to know why they believe what they do.** It's unrealistic to expect young people to share their faith if they don't understand it. How do you know the Bible is reliable? Is there evidence for God? How do you know you're a Christian? Why does God let evil happen in the world? By challenging kids to ask and find answers to these kinds of tough questions, you help their faith grow.

• **Teach kids to share their faith.** Explain the basics of witnessing. Let kids share their faith in the youth group—a "safe" environment. Give them practical tools they can use to reach their friends.

● **Give kids opportunities to share their faith.** It's useless to teach kids the "whys" and "hows" and then not allow them the opportunity to share. Prepare an evangelistic skit to share in a local park. Encourage kids to write notes to friends telling about their faith. If you provide opportunities and challenge kids to reach out to their friends, young people will naturally begin sharing what they believe and encouraging their friends to accept Christ.

A youth minister in Southern California moved to a church with 20 youth group members. The first night, he began sharing his desire for them to win their friends to Jesus. Within three weeks, all but two kids left the program.

But he kept working with those two young people. He encouraged scripture memorization, shared the importance of unconditional love and grounded their faith in the Bible. Before long, those two young people had each led two friends to Christ. That same pattern continued until the church had a strong youth program filled with committed Christian young people.

Missions and Service

Jesus calls Christians to serve others. The Christian life is incomplete when kids receive without giving.

As youth leaders, we need to challenge teenagers to give more money to help a child in Haiti. We need to plant dreams in young people. Not dreams of trips to a mall, but of trips to Mexico to help people in need. And wouldn't it be wonderful to see more teenagers show up to serve in a soup kitchen than to goof off in an amusement park?

The last thing Jesus taught his disciples before his Ascension was about missions. He told them first to be his "witnesses" in their hometown of Jerusalem. Then they were to go to the area around them. Finally, he challenged them to head to the "ends of the earth" (Acts 1:8).

Youth groups in small churches can follow the same pattern. First, take the message to your school and homes. Then take it to the surrounding community—homeless shelters, soup kitchens, crisis-pregnancy centers. Then look beyond to the nation and world.

Every summer, hundreds of youth groups respond to Christ's challenge by taking their message of hope to places of despair. They travel across the country to workcamps to repair homes for low-income and elderly people. And they travel outside the country to Mexico, Haiti and even Africa.

When a youth group reaches out to others, it changes. Young people discover the joy of Christian service. They struggle with questions about their world and how they can make a difference in it. No longer is their faith superficial. Instead, it shapes the way they live.

A youth group in a small Kansas City church was like a lot of suburban youth groups—especially affluent ones. The five or six kids were accustomed to big events such as the annual trip to the Lake of the Ozarks and a day at the Worlds of Fun amusement park. It had always been that way. Sure, other youth workers had tried to break the fun-and-games mentality, but it never worked. Either the leader got frustrated and quit, or the kids stopped coming to anything but social activities.

Then Tara was chosen as the new youth leader.

Tara knew the dynamics of this youth group. But she also felt strongly about the need to stretch these kids in Christian commitment—especially to missions.

The first time she planned a mission trip to a nearby children's home, nobody showed up.

Tara didn't give up. She decided to try piggybacking an exciting activity with a service project. So she planned a weeklong trip to St. Louis. The trip would be fun, including trips to an amusement park, the zoo and a baseball game. But it would also include two days of hard work at an inner-city mission. Kids each had to raise their own finances and also contribute food and clothing for the mission.

A dozen kids signed up!

The small group blossomed to 15 or 20 committed Christian kids with hearts for service. They no longer take many trips to amusement parks and baseball games. Instead, each summer they research and discover a different ministry that needs help. And they spend a week in missions every summer.

Tara is still the youth leader. As she looks back on the past few years, she remembers how hard it was to change those kids. But she figures that if Jesus took three years to get his followers to think more about needs than nets, then the least she could do was stay that long.

In retrospect, it's a good thing she did.

True Success

Sometimes when we're planning and leading youth ministry, we get caught up in the details. How many kids are coming? Do we have enough refreshments? Will kids have fun?

But youth ministry is more than nifty programs and crazy crowdbreakers.

It's watching a 13-year-old girl with "boys on the brain" grow into a young woman willing to go where she's needed in God's kingdom.

It's seeing the clumsy junior high boy who wants to fly in the Air Force become a young man willing to spend his life as a missionary pilot.

It's watching young people who care only about how they look and what they'll do on the weekend learn to care about their world and the people around them.

Those are the real signs of a successful youth ministry. They don't require large numbers at youth group meetings. And they don't require the latest programming gimmick or resource. Rather, they grow out of the love, patience, energy and prayers of youth workers who take time to care.

Endnotes

[1]Dub Ambrose and Walt Mueller, *Ministry to Families With Teenagers* (Loveland, CO: Group Books, 1988), 296-332.

[2]PARENTS & TEENAGERS, Box 482, Mt. Morris, IL 61054.

[3]Larry Keefauver, *Friends and Faith* (Loveland, CO: Group Books, 1986), 17.

CHAPTER 5

Helping Teenagers Become Leaders

C ory, a freshman, plays football and maintains a solid B average in school. He has many other interests, but Cory spends his spare time at church. Why? He's editor of his youth group's newsletter. Every month, he and three other teenagers research, type, lay out and distribute their paper, which they affectionately call Youth Yak.

• • •

Michelle, 17, is a farm kid who has a heart for the poor. She challenges her small church and youth group friends to share what they have. Then once a month, she gathers cans of food and hand-me-down clothes and takes them to a local food bank and thrift shop.

It's not easy work, and Michelle rarely sees those who benefit. But she helps people in need and keeps her congregation concerned about others.

• • •

Kyle, 13, is shy. He doesn't like sports, isn't good in front of a group and sometimes even feels awkward in small group discussions.

But Kyle has a gift to give his youth group: photography. He takes pictures at every youth group event. He shares some with the newsletter editors, and he keeps a scrapbook of all the youth events. Kyle's talent brings a unique dimension to his youth group.

• • •

Such stories are inspiring. We dream of youth groups filled with kids who actively live their faith. We imagine what it might be like to have kids plan and lead meetings, be active members of the congregation and reach out to the world in Christian compassion.

Building leadership among young people is a key to helping them mature into strong Christians. It's also vital for the ongoing health of the youth ministry. Without a core of teenage leaders, youth ministries often crumble when a youth minister leaves.

If we teach kids solid leadership skills, they'll carry those skills with them the rest of their lives. Someday they'll be church leaders. If they develop leadership skills today through their churches, they can have a tremendous impact on their churches and communities in the future.

Thus, building solid youth leadership is more than just a way to fill jobs in your church. It's an important way to help young people grow and mature into Christian leaders.

Small Church Excuses

Most small churches know they need to develop youth leadership. However, when it comes to actually doing it, many hesitate. There are several excuses for not involving kids in leadership:

"We just don't have any kids who can lead worship or teach Sunday school." Maybe not. But who limited leadership to leading worship or teaching Sunday school? Leadership can take many different forms. Granted, some tasks, such as teaching and songleading, require special gifts. But others that are just as important, such as ushering or operating the sound system, don't require those talents. Every young person has something to offer. To say otherwise sells young people short on their abilities.

"All the group leaders have left." In my first month of ministry in one church, I had two senior girls, one junior guy, two sophomore girls and a host of junior highers. By my second month of youth ministry, the two senior girls were too busy elsewhere, the junior boy didn't come anyway, and the two sophomore girls left because of all those junior highers. All my leader kids were gone.

Then along came Flora, a seventh-grader who quickly stepped into leadership. Jason, a bright, spiritually mature eighth-grader, soon followed. Then Jenni. Before long I had new leaders. They weren't necessarily better than the ones I lost. But they became strong leaders for the group.

As long as you have kids, you'll have potential leaders. If you focus on the leaders you lose—as they get busy, go elsewhere or graduate—you miss seeing the leaders-in-the-making.

"But if we let the kids do it, they'll mess up." They will sometimes. But if they never have the opportunity to mess up, they'll never know how to cope with frustration when they fail. Besides, small churches and youth groups will endure—even appreciate—kids' efforts, even if those efforts aren't polished.

This excuse may also reveal an ego problem in the church. If you insist that every program, every game and every activity go flawlessly, you'll suffocate your youth group. If you have great meetings and top-notch games but never allow the teenagers to express their gifts and faith, you may actually hurt the kids—because they'll never learn to use their gifts or cope with inevitable failures.

"Older church members won't accept the kids' leadership." In small churches steeped in tradition, having kids take charge can be a frightening proposition for older members used to the way "we've always done it." They have visions of rock bands, clowns, dances and circus acts replacing the worship and education patterns that have become comfortable for them.

There's some truth to this concern. But you don't have to make radical changes to involve young people. Begin by having them fill small roles traditionally reserved for adults—reading scripture, collecting the offering, serving church dinners, leading devotions. Get the congregation used to having teenagers in leadership.

Then gradually have the young people add creative touches—skits and activities. You'll be surprised how accepting adults will be. A word of caution: Don't tamper with traditions that have particularly deep significance until you're sure the church is ready to participate in a new approach.

"Our kids aren't spiritually mature." Isn't that an excellent reason to encourage kids to be leaders? Anyone who has taught a class or given a speech knows how much you learn when you lead. By challenging kids to take leadership, we also challenge them to grow in their faith and abilities.

No, some kids won't be able to preach. But they may be able to do something simpler—like lead a devotion. No, some kids can't lead Sunday worship now. But they may be able to lead songs for youth group.

"Kids don't want to get their hands dirty." This excuse underestimates young people. In fact, just the opposite may be true. Kids want to be involved and to share their gifts. Kids want to "be somebody"—to have a purpose in life. Just look at the phenomenal growth of youth workcamp programs in recent years. For example, from 1982 to 1989 the number of teenagers participating in Group Workcamps quadrupled from about 1,000 to 4,000. And the number of camps tripled. Kids are hungry for ways to make a difference in the world.

Karen is a 12-year-old who wouldn't take no for an answer. She wanted to feed homeless people in inner-city Miami. Her youth workers expressed concern about the danger. Her pastor suggested she start such a project in her own community (even though few homeless people lived there). Everyone told her to find another ministry.

But Karen wouldn't let go of her dream. She organized a fund-raiser that collected several thousand dollars for an inner-city mission. Through the summer, she worked daily in a soup kitchen.

Today Karen's church has a mission outreach to Miami's homeless. All because Karen didn't mind getting her hands dirty.

Jesus' Model

Even if you're convinced that involving young people in leadership is important, you may have a lot of questions. Where do you start? How do you stretch kids to become leaders?

People probably asked similar questions about Jesus and his disciples. How could Jesus turn a small, motley crew of un-educated fishermen, a tax collector and other assorted misfits into church leaders? But he did it! He entrusted the good news to 12 ordinary people who carried a new, vital message to the ends of the Earth. Let's look at Jesus' ministry to discover some principles for developing leadership in our small church youth groups.

Jesus developed leadership by using everyone, not just a few. Jesus gave *all* his disciples work—whether it was passing out bread and fish to a hungry crowd (Mark 8:6-7) or baptizing new converts (John 4:2). Every disciple was a leader in Jesus' group. So imagine each teenager in your small group as a leader.

Your group may not have all the gifts and abilities you'd like it to have. But all youth group members have leadership potential. They may be able to do something difficult like edit-ing a youth newsletter. Or they may do something as simple as pumping gas on a youth trip.

You may question whether pumping gas is really leader-ship. I believe it is. In fact, I don't distinguish between leader-ship and service. Jesus taught "servant leadership." A true leader serves. And a true servant leads by example.

Lane is special. When the world looks at Lane, it sees a

mentally impaired teenager. Kids often picked on Lane at school and, sadly, even in youth group. But Ron, Lane's youth minister, saw something different. On a youth group trip when the van stopped for gas, Ron encouraged all the kids to help. Three girls eagerly began shining the windows. A couple of the older guys propped up the hood and checked the fluids. Another girl pumped the gas. Amid all the action, Ron noticed Lane still sitting in the van.

"Come help us out, Lane," Ron pleaded.

But Lane just shook his head. He didn't want to help, he mumbled. Ron had a hunch what might be the problem. Lane didn't want to help because he feared ridicule if he failed.

So Ron coaxed Lane out of the van by telling him he had a job just for him. When all the gas was pumped, the windows shined and fluids checked, Ron handed Lane the credit card. Together they paid for the gas.

From that trip on, Lane always paid the cashier. Such confidence by Ron boosted Lane's self-image and gave him the healthy pride of fulfilling an important responsibility.

Jesus realized there are different types of people. Can you imagine having the 12 disciples in your youth group? What a mixture!

First there was Peter. Here's a guy who never knew when to keep his mouth shut. Imagine what he'd be like in a youth group discussion.

Then there were James and John—the "sons of thunder!" They'd play football in school, and they'd always say whatever was on their mind.

Every youth group has an activist, right? Jesus' group did too. In his case it was a fiery young man named Simon the Zealot. Zealots were rebels with a cause. If Simon were in a youth group today, he'd bring petitions for people to sign. And he'd always be challenging his peers to get involved in another cause.

Don't forget Judas Iscariot. A bad apple, right? Well, even old Judas had his job in Jesus' group: treasurer. Jesus even saw potential in the man who later would betray him.

Small churches need to understand that different kids have

different gifts. Take time to know your kids and what they can and can't do. Then give them opportunities to share their talents.

When Mike began doing youth ministry in a small church in Texas, his group didn't seem to have any natural leaders. But Mike noticed Grady—a quiet kid who seemed particularly bright. And the other kids looked up to Grady.

So Mike made it his project to turn Grady into a leader. Mike pushed the teenager to be an upfront, visible leader. He'd ask Grady to lead Bible studies, but Grady always refused.

After several frustrating weeks, Mike realized he had made a mistake. He had assumed a "leader" would fit into a narrow category. So he asked Grady ways he'd like to serve. Grady said he didn't like being in front of the group, but he'd love to help plan programs and do other behind-the-scenes leadership.

Grady began helping Mike prepare Bible studies and meetings. He'd call kids who were absent to make sure they were okay. And when someone new came to a meeting, Mike knew he could count on Grady to sit by and befriend the new person. By learning about and developing Grady's gifts, Mike had a much stronger leader than he could have ever forced Grady to become.

Jesus made leadership fun. Wouldn't it have been great to hand out all that free bread and fish to 5,000 people? Or imagine fishing with Jesus—you'd never know what to expect. One time he'd walk on water. Another time he'd tell you to throw your net on the other side where it would fill to the breaking point. Jesus knew that developing leaders doesn't have to be boring.

No matter what the task, discover ways to make learning fun. Take kids to call on visitors and youth group "strays." The entire group can fit in one vehicle—a feat big groups could never handle! Then cap off the evening at an ice cream shop. Your whole group could fit in one booth for a real family feeling. Let your group teach a Sunday school lesson for one week in all the departments, giving your regular teachers a refreshing break. Schedule planning sessions in the comfort of a volunteer young person's home.

Jesus commended his disciples when they did well. In Matthew 16, Jesus asked his disciples, "Who do people say the Son of Man is?" Well-educated in Sunday school answers, the disciples spouted out what they thought Jesus wanted to hear. John the Baptist. Elijah. Jeremiah. Then Jesus made the question deeply personal: "But what about you? Who do you say I am?" Without hesitation, impetuous Peter blurted out, "You are the Christ, the Son of the living God."

Exactly!

Jesus commended Peter for his answer.

Similarly, you need to affirm your kids. They deserve to know when they've done well. Send notes or make phone calls. Write congratulation announcements for the church newsletter. Post kids' names and deeds on the youth bulletin board. Whatever creative ways you choose, recognize and affirm leadership in your kids.

Small churches have a unique opportunity to affirm kids who aren't often appreciated in a success-oriented world. Kids who may not fit into other places are accepted and given responsibilities in small churches. By affirming them and their gifts, you provide rich soil that helps them blossom into mature Christian leaders.

Affirmation is also important in small churches where group members may get depressed because their program doesn't attract lots of kids. They need to hear that even though the group is smaller, they're just as important as other kids in larger groups.

Jesus allowed his disciples to fail. Let's go back to Peter. Within minutes of Jesus' affirmation for Peter's faith, we find Jesus rebuking Peter (Matthew 16:23). Makes you wonder if Peter would ever get it right! Even though Jesus had just commended Peter for his faith, he didn't try to protect Peter from failure.

That wasn't Peter's first experience with failure either. Remember the time he tried to walk on water (Mark 6:45-52)? Peter certainly took leadership then. The other 11 disciples remained glued to their dry seats. I can imagine Jesus thinking as Peter stepped out onto that water, "Finally, I'm starting to get somewhere with this guy." But then Peter took his eye off the Creator to worry about the creation, and sank.

Peter failed.

Peter had to fail in order to learn and grow, and so do the kids in your youth group. Sure, games might not be as flashy or announcements as polished with kids leading them. But you've got to give kids a chance.

Once I had a group member named Jason who was chosen by the kids to be in charge of all the games for youth group meetings.

Everything went fine—for about two months. Then Jason asked someone else to plan games, and that person didn't show up. A few minutes before meeting time, I asked Jason what games were slated. Jason's face stiffened, then went expressionless.

"Don't you have backup games?" I asked, knowing he didn't.

"What are we going to do, Rick?" Jason countered. "We need something!"

I could tell he was desperate. I also knew there was a lesson in this. It would've been easy for me to improvise. But rescuing Jason wouldn't help him learn responsibility. So I showed him some game books and told him I'd stall until he found something. Five minutes later we were playing a game.

Jason never again missed having a game. He had learned through failure.

Jesus didn't force his disciples into leadership. Jesus didn't push the disciples to follow Peter's courageous attempt to walk on water. Nor did he make Matthew (a tax collector) tend the till instead of Judas Iscariot. Jesus let his disciples assume their natural leadership positions.

Such an approach allowed some disciples to become visible, high-profile leaders. Jesus saw their gifts and emphasized their leadership strengths. His efforts paid off. Peter preached the gospel boldly, while John wrote letters of love and encouragement to early churches. James became one of the first Christian martyrs for expressing his faith (Acts 12:2).

As we support and nurture kids in the leadership they take

in the church, some will naturally assume high-profile leadership positions. We can use their gifts just as we use the leadership gifts kids give behind the scenes.

Jesus constantly maintained his relationship with God. Jesus led by example. And one of his greatest leadership strengths was his prayer life. Before Jesus selected the 12 disciples, he spent an entire night praying alone, asking for God's guidance (Luke 6:12-16).

Because Jesus walked so closely with the Father, his example rubbed off on his disciples. It took three years, a lot of failures and a few headaches. But Jesus' relationship gave his disciples a model to follow.

Our own relationship with God is vital. Because this is such a crucial issue, we'll deal with it in detail in Chapter 9.

Small Church Opportunities

We can involve young people in the church in many different ways. The hard part is figuring out what those things are. Use the "Discovering Kids' Gifts" worksheet (page 76) to begin the process. Also have kids complete the "Hey! I Can Do That!" survey (page 82) to help you discover hidden gifts and talents.

Here are five main areas where young people can actively serve and lead in a small church:

Youth program planning and leadership—Tim is one of those teenagers people listen to. He's great at putting words together and stringing in a joke or two. That's why his youth minister asked him to give the youth announcements every Sunday morning. His witty style helps people know—and remember—opportunities in the youth program.

Young people with a knack for organization and group leadership can lead group meetings, plan activities, prepare socials and games, organize and decorate the youth room, edit a newsletter or do any other leadership tasks.

In one church, we set up four leadership "families" in the youth group: the social family, the publicity family, the spiritual-life family and the secretarial/financial family. Every youth group member was asked to choose a family. Then each

Discovering Kids' Gifts

Instructions: Use this three-step process to discover ways kids can use their gifts in your church's ministry.

1. List group members' names and phone numbers in the left column.

2. In the center column, write everything you know that they do well. Include specific talents (playing guitar), hobbies (collecting baseball cards) and personal qualities (patience). If you give the "Hey! I Can Do That!" survey, include items from it as well.

3. Then, in the third column, list specific responsibilities in the church or youth group that parallel that teenager's talents or interests.

4. Keep the list handy, and use it to recruit teenagers for different responsibilities.

Name and Phone Number	Talents and Interests	Matching Church Responsibilities

continued

Discovering Kids' Gifts (continued)

Name and Phone Number	Talents and Interests	Matching Church Responsibilities

family—supervised by an adult volunteer—met monthly (outside youth meeting times) for fellowship and planning.

The social family took care of games at youth group meetings, as well as all social events. The publicity family made posters and got the word out about our programs. The spiritual-life family worked on finding service projects, discovering personal needs and organizing a youth group prayer chain. The secretarial/financial family kept the books, collected money for an overseas project, found ways to finance the youth program and organized fund-raisers. The end result was a youth program that could run without a youth minister.

Even a group of four kids could organize this way, with each young person taking one responsibility.

Service—Cindy can't really sing. She's not much for games. She usually sits in the back pew of her small church. If you ask her to pray or share in a discussion, you'll probably be met with silence. Cindy doesn't get actively involved—at least not in those ways.

Rather, Cindy does jobs no one else wants to do. She picks up leftover bulletins after worship services. Or she washes communion cups. You don't *see* Cindy do a lot. But when Cindy's around, a lot gets done.

Kids in small churches have more opportunities to serve in the church than kids in larger churches. Since small churches don't have as many people to do all the jobs, willing teenagers can be godsends. And the kids will really be appreciated for what they do. They can type bulletins, do maintenance work, operate the sound system, answer the office phone and do dozens of other jobs.

Have the youth group lead worship services at a local nursing home. Bake cookies and carol at a home for severely retarded children. Do church workdays to clean the grounds. Organize a food or clothing drive for low-income people in your community. Attend a workcamp to rebuild homes for low-income and elderly people. Involvement in service can make a difference in kids' lives—and in the lives of the people they touch.

Worship—Some kids have abilities in specific areas to use in worship, such as music, drama, puppets or clowning. Encourage young people to use these gifts to create worship experiences for the church and the youth group.

Lynnette loves music. Before coming to a small church, Lynnette warmed a pew in a large church that relied on adults for special music. But then her family moved and decided to attend a small church.

The congregation is delighted when Lynnette sings—which she does about once a month. She also leads a children's choir, which she started. And recently, the pastor asked her to help select music for Sunday services. Lynnette now feels at home in the church. She feels as though she's contributing.

Education—Older kids can assist in Sunday school or vacation Bible school. Or they can work in the church nursery. There are probably jobs for young people in any educational program your church offers. Often teenagers get as much or more out of teaching younger kids as they'd get out of being students.

Church leadership—Cassandra and Nadine like to organize special events. Along with four adults in their small church, they serve on the food committee that organizes fellowship dinners, Easter sunrise breakfasts and special meals for traveling music teams. It's not a glamorous job. Often they're the last to eat—and always the last to leave. But they enjoy their ministry in the church.

Including young people in the church's leadership isn't as difficult as it may seem. Church committees generally welcome young people with a willingness to serve. And many of the church's ministries can be accomplished just as well by someone who's 16 as by someone who's 60.

Small Church Involvement

Once you've overcome the hesitations and discovered the opportunities, it's time to get kids involved. Use this six-step process for giving kids responsibilities in the church.

1. Identify needed gifts. What special abilities, if any, does a particular job or role require? Can the job be learned quickly, or does the person need natural abilities to do the job well?

Sometimes we're tempted to give kids any jobs that need getting done. However, if a young person doesn't fit the job, the results will be discouraging for everyone. The young person may be frustrated because he or she feels inadequate.

When you determine the gifts needed, write a job description. It doesn't need to be fancy, but it should include basic information about the job. What are the responsibilities and expectations? How much time will it take? How long will the job last? What type of support and training can the young person expect?

2. Recruit young people. Once you've determined the gifts needed for a particular responsibility, look for the appropriate young person for the task. Use the results from your "Discovering Kids' Gifts" worksheet (page 76) and the "Hey! I Can Do That!" survey (page 82) to come up with names.

When you think of a person who might be appropriate, ask yourself:

• Can this young person do the job effectively?
• Is the young person reliable enough for the job?
• Is this responsibility the best way to use the young person's gifts?
• What factors might make it unwise to give this responsibility to this young person?

If the answers to these questions are satisfactory, approach the young person. Explain the responsibility, and give him or her a copy of the job description. Answer any questions he or she has; then give the teenager time to think about the offer.

If the young person accepts the offer, start planning together.

If the young person turns down the offer, respect that decision. Find out why, and ask if there are other responsibilities he or she might be interested in. Keep notes on any ideas he or she has.

You can also get kids involved by learning about their abilities, then finding ways to use those skills in the church. Beyond the obvious examples of music or drama, think of creative ways to put different skills to work, such as the following:

• If someone's interested in farming or agriculture, have him or her do landscaping and yardwork around the church. Or encourage the young person to volunteer to help elderly people plant their own gardens.

• A teenager who works on cars might offer to give free oil changes to needy church members. Or he or she could be responsible for car maintenance on youth group outings.

• If someone enjoys cooking, ask him or her to help in the church kitchen. Or suggest that the teenager help with a Meals On Wheels program or a soup kitchen.

• Ask artistic teenagers to design banners for your sanctuary or posters for publicity.

• If a teenager has skills in architecture, encourage him or her to build a miniature model of your church. Not only will it be fun for people to talk about, but it will help newcomers learn their way around the facility.

• A young person who enjoys interior design could certainly decorate the youth group meeting area. Or he or she could help design other church rooms such as the nursery and children's classrooms.

3. Plan together. Work with the young person to begin the planning process. Ask questions such as:

• What specific things must be done to accomplish the task?

• If training is needed, how will it take place and when will it begin?

• Who else needs to be involved in the planning?

With the young person, develop a specific action plan. Decide on specific dates and goals. Recruit additional help if it's needed.

4. Train the young person. For most jobs, training needs to be more than a one-time meeting or lecture. It should involve long-term support and encouragement. The process—which is outlined in J. David Stone's book, *Catching the Rainbow: The Complete Youth Ministries Handbook, Volume 2*—goes like this:

Hey! I Can Do That!

Instructions: We need you to be involved in our church. Complete the following survey to help us out. Check any areas where you have talent and/or interest. We'll use your responses to involve you in future programs, activities and projects. Thanks.

Name: _____

Address: _____

Phone: _____

☐ Art
☐ Teaching
☐ Puppets
☐ Organization/
   planning
☐ Electronics
☐ Computers

☐ Photography
☐ Drama
☐ Writing
☐ Cooking
☐ Work/service
   projects
☐ Camping/
   outdoors

☐ Vocal music (What part? _____)
☐ Instrumental music (What instrument? _____)
☐ Sports/athletics (List: _____)
☐ Other (Explain: _____)

If I could share one talent or ability with the youth group, it would be:

Hobbies I enjoy:

- First I do it, and you watch.
- Then we both do it.
- Then you do it, and I support you.
- Finally, you do it, and I move on.[1]

5. Support and consult. Once training is complete and the young person is doing the job well, don't leave him or her alone. Offer regular encouragement. Call to see if he or she needs resources or ideas. Find out about any problems, and offer suggestions. Check progress on the goals you set.

6. Evaluate. After the young person has completed the leadership responsibility, evaluate. Discuss what went well and what could be improved. Affirm the teenager, and find out what other responsibilities he or she might enjoy.

Small Church Results

"Curly" was an eighth-grader when his youth leader started encouraging him to get involved in leadership. At first, it was scary for Curly. Some tasks required praying aloud and leading short devotionals—which he'd never been trained to do.

But Curly wanted to get involved. Even though his voice cracked, he led hymns during morning worship. He and a friend visited shut-ins. And he led the group to start its first newsletter.

Curly's leadership in his church changed his life. He committed himself to full-time Christian service. Today he's a full-time youth minister. If you ask Curly what made the difference, he won't mention a particular program. He won't point to any youth trip. Rather, Curly will point back to the youth leaders who gave him a chance to make a difference.

I know Curly well, because Curly's story is my story. My life was changed because my church was willing to let kids get involved in leadership.

Endnotes

[1] J. David Stone, *Catching the Rainbow: The Complete Youth Ministries Handbook, Volume 2* (Nashville, TN: Abingdon Press, 1981), 18.

CHAPTER 6

Recruiting Volunteers in the Small Church

O nce a professional football coach took aside his recruiter after a strenuous, late-summer practice. The recruiter's lousy picks were rapidly ruining the team, so the coach wanted to share his distaste for the recruiter's job performance.

The coach had the recruiter watch a game film of college prospects. After watching a few minutes, the coach began, "Does our team want a guy who gets knocked down all the time?"

"No sir," the recruiter replied confidently.

"That's right. Does our team want a guy who gets knocked down and then gets back up?"

Figuring the coach was making a point, the recruiter answered no.

"Right again, my friend," the coach shot back, obviously gaining momentum. "Now, does our team want a guy who's knocked down and gets back up, is knocked down again and gets back up and is decked a third time and gets back up?"

"Yes, sir!" the recruiter exclaimed. "That's who we want!"

"Wrong!" the coach yelled. "I want the player who's doing the knocking down!"

● ● ●

Like football recruiters, youth leaders need to find the right people. But too often we're like the recruiter in the story—we don't know what to look for.

Sometimes we're so desperate we recruit anyone who'll sign up. Or we recruit people we personally like, even if they aren't the right people. Or we might recruit lots of people, all with the same gifts. So our youth ministries are like football teams made up of only quarterbacks or tackles.

In other situations, we look around the congregation and conclude there's no one who can do the job. So we do the work ourselves. In each case, the result is we work with an incomplete or imbalanced team.

How do you recruit a strong youth ministry team in a small church? It's not always easy. Most active church members are involved in other leadership roles in the church. Thus, finding adults who can commit significant time to youth ministry can be difficult.

But recruiting volunteers is also rewarding. By taking time to enlist quality volunteers, you not only see the effect their ministries have on the teenagers in your youth group, but you also give them opportunities to use their talents and abilities.

Why People Don't Volunteer

Before we discuss the "hows" of recruiting, we need to understand why it's sometimes hard to find willing volunteers. The list of reasons people have for not doing volunteer work is often long. They mention family conflicts, lack of skills, other responsibilities and on and on.

But regardless of how long the list grows, most of the reasons fall into one of three categories:

Reason #1: People aren't asked. You might be surprised how many people would gladly contribute to the youth program if someone would ask. Yet they sit on the sidelines while we rely on ourselves and a few burned-out helpers who complain that no one's willing to pitch in.

Youth workers in small churches don't seek volunteers for a variety of reasons.

• We think we can do it alone. In his book *Great Ideas for Small Youth Groups*, Wayne Rice describes the problem this way: "One inherent danger of a small youth group is the tendency to think that because the group is small, it can be handled by only one person. This isn't true. Regardless of how small a youth group might be, it provides an ideal setting for the development of a team ministry—a group of willing adults who do together what none of them can do alone."[1]

• Recruiting is hard work, and it takes time—time we don't think we have. We justify to ourselves that it's easier and quicker to do the work ourselves than to find and train someone else to do it. But this attitude is shortsighted.

Jesus could have spent all his time healing or doing other direct ministry. But he recruited and trained his disciples to continue his ministry when he was gone. His leaders didn't fall apart when he left—they changed the world.

One particularly busy fall, Janet had trouble finding time to recruit volunteers for her small church's annual youth group retreat. As the weekend approached, she decided it would just be easier to plan the whole event herself. So she found a retreat site, designed the program, did the publicity, contacted a guest speaker, prepared the food—everything.

Everything seemed to be going well until that weekend. So many kids had signed up they had to take two cars. The other driver got lost because he didn't know how to get to the retreat center.

When everyone finally arrived, Janet had to do everything—leading sessions, solving problems, making the speaker feel welcome, even cooking the food. The other adults who volunteered at the last minute were willing to help. But they didn't know anything about the retreat's focus. So Janet left the event frustrated, tired and mad at her own shortsightedness.

• We feel insecure. Once my youth leaders asked if they could take over the group's programming. My first thought was: "You guys can't lead the group like I can. You don't know as much."

But after I peeled my deflated ego off the ground, I realized that my response was reactive. They knew what to do—maybe better than I did. Allowing them to take leadership in the youth program freed me to pursue other ministries.

Giving other people responsibilities also gives them control. New people have new ideas—some of which might seem threatening. Sometimes we feel safer if we keep all the responsibility and control to ourselves. But while that approach may be comfortable, it's not healthy for the church, the youth group or ourselves.

Sometimes we also feel insecure asking other people to do jobs we don't understand. We're afraid we won't be able to answer people's questions about the work. So we don't ask.

• We don't have a long-range vision. Either we're so busy with day-to-day programs we don't think beyond the next meeting's program, or we don't think we'll ever reap the benefits of any planning. So we may say to ourselves, "Well, I'm only here for a little while. Why should I spend all my time training when I could be working with the kids?"

But the question is the answer! Someday you'll probably pass the youth program leadership to other people. When that happens, will you leave a strong ministry that meets the kids' needs? Only if you recruit and train strong volunteers.

Recruiting and training a solid core of volunteers is a long-term process. The efforts rarely pay off quickly; instead, the training is an investment for the future.

• We think we're the only ones qualified. My reason for not recruiting volunteers was always: "Well, the kids need me. If I let someone else do the job, the kids will start turning to that person instead. And that's not right, because I'm the youth minister!"

Such pride cost me many excellent volunteers. Youth ministry isn't a solo act. It's team ministry. Working together is the only way to provide a well-rounded, lasting ministry.

• We don't know how. Often in small churches, youth leaders haven't learned how to recruit volunteers and delegate responsibilities. Many volunteers have always been the ones who are *assigned* tasks, not the ones who assign them to others. And youth workers with training usually have learned to do various jobs, not to empower other people to do them.

Reason #2: People don't have time. Everyone's busy these days. Many people are overcommitted to tasks of work, school and home. And active members of small churches are usually involved in numerous ministries, adding to their busy schedules. As Steve Burt writes in *Activating Leadership in the Small Church,* "Small church folks often feel like the outnumbered Alamo volunteers—overworked, underpaid, asked to fight overwhelming odds in a no-win situation."[2] When we ask them to volunteer for the youth program, they often plead they're already overcommitted.

In his previous church, Chuck was a committed volunteer youth worker. But when he moved and joined a small church, Chuck suddenly found he was needed in numerous church ministries. Within a year, he was elected deacon, had served as church treasurer and was a Sunday school teacher for the young couples' class. When the youth leader asked Chuck to help with the youth program too, he had to say no. He simply didn't have any more time.

Lack of time may be a legitimate reason for not getting involved in youth ministry. Youth ministry is a major commitment, and unless someone can dedicate himself or herself to the program, that person may not be an appropriate volunteer.

But you can provide ways busy people can participate in the youth ministry. Here are three examples:

1. Ask the person to make youth ministry a priority for a future year. Just because someone can't commit to youth ministry now doesn't mean he or she wouldn't be interested in the future. Get a commitment now so he or she will keep the calendar clear next time.

2. Ask people to volunteer for smaller tasks. Many people—particularly young adults—prefer volunteering for jobs that don't involve months of commitment. Find ways to divide tasks into more manageable chunks. For example, instead of asking Sharon to coordinate refreshments for the year's meetings, ask her to provide refreshments for one month. Instead of asking Carl to do a devotion for every youth group meeting,

invite him to lead devotions at your fall retreat.

3. Tell people exactly what's expected. Sometimes they don't realize a particular job won't take much time. If you provide realistic job descriptions that show exactly what time commitment is involved, some people may see they do have time.

Reason #3: People are afraid. The final reason people don't volunteer is fear. This fear takes several forms:

• Fear of commitment—Small churches are notorious for trapping people for life once they've committed to a responsibility. If Margie becomes a youth sponsor, everyone assumes that Margie will always be a youth sponsor. As a result, many people shy away from *any* commitments.

Therefore, it's important to spell out clearly what's expected of volunteers and to limit the time of service. A volunteer job description (such as the "Sample Volunteer Job Description" on page 90) is a good tool for easing this fear.

• Fear of kids—In small churches with older memberships, some people think they're too old and can no longer relate to kids. "I'm not as young as I used to be," moans a woman in her 50s. "Kids want youth leaders who really understand their world."

Sometimes a small group can be even more frightening for these people than a large one. They realize they won't be able to keep a distance from the kids—they'll have to relate to kids on a one-to-one basis.

While kids do need leaders who relate to them and their world, teenagers also need adult leaders who are mature and understanding. The best youth leaders are people who—regardless of age—are willing to listen to and support young people. By introducing these people to teenagers in a non-threatening environment such as an all-church picnic or dinner, you can show them how interesting it can be to get to know your kids.

• Fear of rejection—"What if the kids don't like me?" Some adults don't want to risk rejection by working with teenagers. They're afraid kids will laugh at their mistakes or say things about them after the meeting.

Sample Volunteer Job Description

Thank you for taking the time to involve yourself with our young people. Your commitment and dedication will no doubt influence youth group members. Yes, your time and talents will be taxed. But your efforts won't go unrewarded. Here are a few expectations we have of you as a volunteer youth worker:

We expect you as a youth worker . . .

• to help provide a well-balanced, well-planned program of activities, learning and fellowship.

• to participate in all youth ministry planning and training events. Regular planning meetings usually take place on: _____

• to be prepared for all youth group activities, meetings and programs in which you have responsibilities. If you can't attend a particular program, you'll be expected to find a substitute.

• to be willing to personally involve yourself with the young people in your group through regular phone calls and visits. You're their *minister!*

• to serve wholeheartedly—with a Christlike mind and actions—for *two* years.

• to pray for the church, the youth ministry, the young people and the leaders.

In return for your commitment, you will receive . . .

• inclusion in all youth ministry activities, events, planning and programming.

• training and resources in youth ministry to equip you to carry out your responsibilities.

• assurance that you're being lifted up in prayer for your efforts with the youth program.

Other agreements and expectations:

Youth leader's signature: _____
Volunteer's signature: _____
Date: _____

What these adults need to hear is that kids notice less about how perfectly you run a program and more about how much you care about them. Once again, in the small church, relationships are much more important than having a polished program. Sure, they may kid you about your foibles. But a good sense of humor will make the teasing enjoyable.

• Fear of inadequacy—"I don't know if I know enough to teach or lead a Bible study. What if I get in and can't hack it?" Some people feel unprepared for the tasks youth workers propose. They feel they've failed if only one or two kids show up for a meeting they're leading. And they may fear that the approaches they remember from the "old days" wouldn't work with today's young people.

This is a legitimate concern for potential leaders—particularly those without youth ministry experience, which is common in small churches. Four responses to their concerns can ease the fears:

1. Assure the potential volunteer you'll provide resources and training. Then provide them through workshops, books and magazines. Introduce volunteers to the inexpensive resources in the resource listing on page 164.

2. Always be available to answer questions and offer support.

3. Create a "volunteer in training" program in which you match a veteran with a novice. For one year, have the new person work with the veteran in different jobs. Then he or she will feel more confident when it's time to take charge.

4. Work with other local churches to provide training. (See Chapter 8 for more on networking.)

How to Recruit Volunteers

Recruiting volunteers in a small church is quite different from recruiting in larger churches. On the one hand, everyone knows everyone else in a small church. That can make it easy to find the right person. On the other hand, church leaders tend to rely on a handful of people, often ignoring the hidden talents of other church members. Or they simply find the youngest couple in the church, and assume those people would be good youth leaders—which may or may not be true. And sometimes group members' parents are the only ones asked.

How can you overcome these recruitment problems in small churches? In an article in GROUP Magazine, veteran youth worker Les Christie suggests six general ways to recruit youth ministry volunteers:[3]

The public-appeal method—This well-worn method has many variations. Ask for volunteers from the pulpit, explaining the need and asking volunteers to see you after the service. Write appeal notices in your church newsletter, suggesting people call you if they're interested. Beg for help on your knees in front of adult Sunday school classes. Hang up "wanted posters" to attract people's attention. Shove fliers under windshield wipers in the church parking lot. Do anything to let people know you need help.

The problem with the public-appeal method is that people never know if you're talking to them. A generic "Hey, we need help!" causes few hands to fly into the air. After all, people reason, somebody else will step forward, so why should I? So no one volunteers, and the prodding is wasted.

Sometimes, though, public appeals do work. Some of my best volunteers have been people who responded to a poster's plea or a newsletter's nudge. So you probably shouldn't abandon the public appeal; but don't rely solely on it either.

The telephone method—Need a volunteer? Open the church directory and start calling—randomly.

This method can be discouraging, but it can work well. It's more personal than a letter or poster, and you can discover people you might never have considered for youth ministry.

Be careful about calling at bad times, such as mealtimes. And have a job outline in front of you as you talk.

The volunteer-recruiter method—The best person to recruit new volunteers is an active volunteer. An active volunteer knows the job first-hand. This person can report the frustrations and difficulties of being a volunteer. On the flip side, he or she will also share what motivates them to continue youth work.

I find this method particularly effective. Lay volunteers tend to know the congregation better than staff people do. They know the people who volunteered for youth work five and 10 years ago—people who might give it another try.

The come-and-find-out method—Mary was a potential youth worker at a small church in California. The youth minister had asked her several times to volunteer, but each time Mary said no.

Recently the leader made her pitch again. But this time she gave Mary an option. "Just join us this week for the youth group meeting," she suggested. "If you don't feel comfortable after watching a meeting, I'll leave you alone. But I think you'd be great for the group."

That week, Mary went to the meeting. Almost immediately she realized that working with the youth group was something she should've done a lot sooner. It was nothing like she expected.

Having potential volunteers experience your program is a great way to attract attention to the need. Many churchgoers don't volunteer because they never see how they are needed.

The church leadership method—This method essentially relies on church leaders to develop a pool of potential names. And it can work well. Sometimes church members tell leaders they'd like to work in a particular ministry. Your request for names can jog the leaders' memories.

Augment the leaders' personal knowledge by conducting an interest survey, such as the "How I Can Help" survey on page 94. Keep the results on file, and refer to them when you're looking for volunteers.

The one-to-one method—The final method is the most personal, and it can be one of the most effective, particularly since everyone knows everyone in a small church. Personally contact potential volunteers, explain the job and ask them to join your youth ministry team. People feel honored when a leader makes a request in person. And they often accept the challenge. However, be sure people have an opportunity to turn you down when you use this approach. Otherwise you

How I Can Help

Instructions: Please complete this survey for our youth ministry program. Completing this survey doesn't sign you up for anything. Rather, it gives us a pool of names to work with in the future. We'll contact you when the need arises. Thanks for your time.

Name: _____

Address: _____

Phone: _____

I'm interested in serving the youth program in the following ways (check all that apply):

☐ Serving as a volunteer youth leader (preferred age group: _____)
☐ Hosting youth group events
☐ Helping prepare meals for special events
☐ Preparing and serving refreshments at youth group meetings
☐ Helping with secretarial work such as typing letters, mailing publicity, filing papers
☐ Being a driver for youth group activities
☐ Accompanying music for youth group programs (what instrument? _____)
☐ Leading a home Bible study for teenagers
☐ Transporting teenagers in my neighborhood to the church for youth group activities
☐ Making a special monetary contribution to the youth program
Specific ministry you'd like to support (if any):

_____

How much you'd like to contribute: $_____
☐ Other ways you'd be interested in working with the church's youth ministry program: _____

_____

could have a reluctant, uncommitted volunteer.

Each of these methods can have its place in your recruitment plan. Some people will be attracted by a poster; others won't respond until you personally ask for their help. Thus, the best recruitment method is to combine several methods to attract volunteers.

When You Find the Right People

Someone once said, "The church is full of willing people: Some are willing to work, and the others are willing to let them."

Recruiting volunteers in a small church is finding volunteers who fit the first category. It does little good to tell potential volunteers youth ministry won't take much time or energy. It will. But when you find people who'll accept the challenge of working with young people, your ministry—and theirs—will flourish.

Endnotes

[1] Wayne Rice, *Great Ideas for Small Youth Groups* (Grand Rapids, MI: Zondervan Publishing House, 1986), 29.

[2] Steve Burt, *Activating Leadership in the Small Church* (Valley Forge, PA: Judson Press, 1988), 52.

[3] Les Christie, "In Search of Volunteers," GROUP Magazine (September 1988), 9-11.

CHAPTER 7

Budgeting for Your Youth Ministry

A GROUP Magazine survey found more than one-third of small churches operate their entire youth ministry program with no money from the congregational budget. The rest of the small churches revealed annual budgets of between $50 and $1,500.[1]

The survey confirmed what you already know: Except in a few rare cases, funding for youth ministry in small churches is limited.

I vividly remember the sinking feeling I had when the dreams in my heart didn't match the bucks in the budget. And often it wasn't that the church didn't *want* to support the youth program financially. It simply couldn't.

Most small churches have small incomes that can't meet the many financial needs. The laws of finances work against the smaller church. A monthly mortgage that would be normal for a church with 400 members can become an albatross for a 100-member church, draining its budget.

There are ways to overcome budget frustrations. They involve flexibility, creativity, careful planning and a well-prepared youth ministry budget.

Budget Benefits

Many small churches operate without congregational budgets (much less youth ministry budgets). Each Sunday morning, they collect an offering to cover expenses. And if the first collection doesn't gather enough, they might pass the plate again and again—until they've collected what they need. As long as the Sunday offering covers immediate expenses, the status quo is fine.

Such an approach may pay the bills, but it doesn't fulfill many of the following purposes for creating a budget. And it often keeps the church from supporting youth ministry because other expenses seem more urgent. A church budget that includes youth ministry has numerous advantages.

A budget shows commitment to youth ministry. Having a youth ministry budget symbolizes the church's commitment to youth ministry. Rich Bimler writes in GROUP Magazine: "A church's financial involvement in youth ministry is usually in direct proportion to its youth ministry's effectiveness. A church's financial support of its youth ministry is generally an indicator of how much the adults care about their youth."[2] As Jesus said, "For where your treasure is, there your heart will be also" (Matthew 6:21).

A budget creates accountability. This reason alone should convince small churches with limited money to have a budget. Without a budget, a church or youth program might spend all its money on up-to-date video equipment, then not have enough money to pay for regular expenses.

A budget sets limits on spending so expenditures won't exceed income. At times, I've decided not to buy a resource— even if I really needed it—in order to stay within the budget.

A budget organizes the program. Even if your church doesn't require a breakdown of your youth ministry budget, it's important to itemize expenses within the program. A budget disciplines you to plan your youth program on paper. To decide how much money you need, you have to set priorities in your ministry. Once you've budgeted for curriculum, youth trips, meetings, special events and other needs, you've set helpful parameters for deciding what to do in the coming year.

The Budget Process

When youth workers realize the importance of a youth ministry budget, many immediately jump into the fiscal lake with both feet. They scribble notes and pull files. They check needs and draw up lists. Eventually (if they don't drown in confusing paper work first) they pull all the pieces together and present a massive budget at the next church board meeting. And the budget's shot down.

Such a scenario doesn't have to happen. If your church hasn't had a youth ministry budget before, use the suggestions in the "Getting Support for Your Budget" box to help your congregation see the need to support the ministry. Then use these six simple steps to make your budgeting process go smoothly:

Step 1: Learn the church's budget history. Before you begin planning your budget, be sure you know the dynamics of budgeting in your congregation.

Discover how much your church has spent on youth ministry in the past five to 10 years. This history will help you know what might be a realistic budget request. For example, if your church spent only $400 on youth ministry each year for the past six years and you ask for $2,000 for next year, you'll probably not get it. You'll have to adjust your figures dramatically to have any chance of getting a budget passed.

Also find out exactly what the youth ministry budget covers. Many strange things get put in youth ministry budgets—vacation Bible school supplies, missions offerings and almost anything else. In one church, I thought I had $500 for a youth trip, only to learn the money had already been spent sending children to summer camp. The church had always used youth ministry funds for that purpose, so I didn't really have access to those funds.

Finally, learn who oversees youth ministry expenditures. Is it the youth minister? the senior minister? an elder or deacon? the church treasurer? Knowing who holds the key to the financial vault can prevent miscommunication and misunder-

Getting Support for Your Budget

If your church has never had a youth ministry budget, use these suggestions by Rich Bimler to get started:[3]

1. Begin slowly. It's better to get a little funding than ask for the world and get nothing. It may take a while to convince small church leadership that a youth ministry budget is important.

2. Advocate youth ministry. Show the young people's needs. Share your vision of where the ministry could go with proper funding.

3. Stress the importance of having young people involved in the church. Remember, kids aren't just tomorrow's church; they're also part of today's church.

4. Encourage young people to be involved. Their active participation and leadership will show adults the value of a strong youth ministry.

5. Stress youth ministry as a regular part of the church budget. Remind the church that it supports other ministries as part of the regular budget.

6. Be concerned that the church adequately supports other ministries as well. Go to bat for senior citizens or other church programs. By making sure no one is left out of the budget, you can win some friends for your cause.

7. Discuss your plans and goals with the pastor. Ask for support for including youth ministry in the budget.

8. Encourage kids to give to the church. The church will be more likely to support the youth program if the kids support and are active in the church.

standing when you make your proposal.

Step 2: Gather financial records. Knowing how much various ministries have cost in the past helps you estimate future expenses. Dig up any records you have from previous years. Ask the church treasurer for other records that might be available.

Step 3: Set ministry goals. Develop year-long and long-term goals for your ministry. Without these goals, you won't be able to include new programs or emphases in your ministry. If, for example, you want group members to participate in a denominational leadership training program, you'll need to set aside appropriate funds.

As you discuss goals, include adult volunteers, youth group members, parents and church staff in the planning process. Set priorities for your goals based on your ministry vision (see Chapter 3).

Step 4: Prepare your budget. Don't wait until the last minute to plan your budget. You're likely to leave out important needs, and your estimates of future expenses probably won't be accurate. Moreover, you may be tempted simply to add a few dollars to the previous year's budget—which only perpetuates previous programs without any evaluating or priority-setting.

Preparing a budget doesn't have to be complicated, particularly in a small church. Here's a simple process to adapt to your situation:

1. List each expenditure from the previous year on a separate 3x5 card. Include the name of the expense (such as "food for fall retreat") and the total amount.

2. Arrange your cards into logical categories based on your ministry emphases. For example, you could use the following categories:
- Resources/Training;
- Special Events; and
- Activities.

3. Transfer the information from the 3x5 cards to a "Budget Worksheet" such as the one on page 102. Here's a sample of how the worksheet might look for the "Resources" category:

Category: Resources	This Year's Expenses	Next Year's Anticipated Expenses	Proposed Budget
a. Books and magazines	#125.00		
b. Films and videos	#50.00		
c. Sunday school Curriculum	#105.00		
TOTAL	#280.00		

4. Begin projecting preliminary budget figures for the next year. Write amounts in the "Next Year's Anticipated Expenses" column. Don't worry about the number being too high right now. You're just establishing a starting point. If, in your planning, you set goals to add new ministries, add these to the list as well. Your sheet will look something like this:

Category: Resources	This Year's Expenses	Next Year's Anticipated Expenses	Proposed Budget
a. Books and magazines	#125.00	# 150.00	
b. Films and videos	#50.00	# 100.00	
c. Sunday school Curriculum	# 105.00	# 115.00	
d. Music resources	$ 0.00	$50.00	
TOTAL	#280.00	# 415.00	

5. When you've assigned a cost projection for each need in the "Next Year's Anticipated Expenses" column, total the whole column.

If you're like most budgeters, the figure will seem outrageously high. The first time I budgeted a whole year in advance, the total exceeded the previous year's budget by $2,500. I felt doomed. No budget committee would pass such an increase. So I went on to the next step.

Budget Worksheet

Category:	This Year's Expenses	Next Year's Anticipated Expenses	Proposed Budget
Total			
Revenue Resources			
Deficit or Surplus			

6. Analyze, trim and rearrange your projections.

• First highlight essential expenses on the list (such as curriculum and building expenses).

• Evaluate which other items could be trimmed and still be acceptable. For example, you might prefer to have $400 for the summer trip, but you think you could make the trip work with $350. Write the new amount in a different color above your original estimate.

• Examine your list again and set priorities. Which areas of funding are most important? least important? Circle the items that could be cut if necessary.

7. Use your adjustments to fill out the last column—your proposed budget. Set realistic and workable amounts in each category. If necessary, delete items you believe could be cut. Or propose them as above-and-beyond challenges for the church to support.

Your sheet should look something like this:

Category: Resources	This Year's Expenses	Next Year's Anticipated Expenses	Proposed Budget
a. Books and magazines	$125.00	$~~150.00~~ $140.00	$140.00
b. Films and videos	$50.00	$~~100.00~~ $75.00	$75.00
c. Sunday school curriculum	$105.00	$115.00	$115.00
d. Music resources	$0.00	$~~50.00~~ $40.00	$40.00
TOTAL	$280.00	$~~415.00~~ $370.00	$370.00

8. Re-evaluate your proposal in light of your ministry goals. Does the budget reflect your priorities and needs? If not, adjust the figures appropriately.

Step 5: Present your budget proposal. The numbers on your budget proposal will mean little to the church board without explanation. Thus it's important to explain in person your needs and the costs. Not only can your presentation help your budget allocation, but it can be a valuable opportunity to share your youth ministry vision with the congregation.

If the budget you propose looks much bigger than the previous year, decide how to promote the increase to the church. The first time I used this process, I made a few cuts but realized the youth program had been grossly underfinanced.

So after revisions, I decided to champion the budget increase. I used graphs and statistics to emphasize the need. And I showed how the proposed amount would enhance the ministry. The proposal passed.

When you propose your budget, support your needs with reasons. If you need $200 for Sunday school curriculum, give solid reasons why the material you want to purchase meets the group's needs. If you want $75 for postage, explain the costs of mailing your youth newsletter and other items.

Finally, while it's important to stand behind your request, it's just as important to be flexible. If the whole church is tightening its budgetary belt, look for ways to cut expenses in the youth department. If board members don't understand or are skeptical about a particular budget request, ask for their ideas.

Stan works in a congregation of 90 near Denver. While debating a budget proposal, some board members had difficulty justifying the amount Stan wanted for refreshments. Stan explained why he needed the refreshments, what he was buying and how much it cost each week.

When Stan finished the explanation, a deacon responded: "I guess you didn't know this, but I own a bakery. If it'll help, I'll donate two dozen cookies every week."

Because he listened to the concerns, explained his needs and was flexible, Stan never again had to request money for refreshments.

Step 6: Keep track of expenses. Once you have a budget in place, keep good records of your expenses and income through the year. If you didn't budget enough in some areas, keep notes on unmet needs. If you found you didn't need all the money you budgeted for another area, note those surpluses as well.

One simple way to keep track is to collect the receipts in a file. Then when you prepare the next year's budget, you can see if you need to add other items to the budget.

Alternative Funding

What if the church board decides not to include youth ministry in the church budget? What if the approved budget is inadequate for your expenses? Or what if you want to have special ministries beyond the budget? Then you need to find additional sources of income. Here are a few possibilities:

Have the kids support the program themselves. Fundraisers, annual dues and individual contributions by group members can help pay for activities and programming. Many small churches use this approach effectively. The "Tips for Successful Fund-Raisers" box on page 106 lists several suggestions for making your fund-raisers successful.

Solicit donations from church members. Create a list of needs for the coming year and calculate anticipated costs. Then ask church members to donate money to support the program. If, for example, you need $1,500, and you work in a 100-member church, you'll need an average of $15 from each person to support the program (or $50 each from 30 people or $100 each from 15 people).

A similar option is to distribute commitment cards and ask people to pledge a certain amount to the youth program—either as a one-time gift or an ongoing commitment.

Find low-cost programming. Commit yourself to activities and programming that cost nickels and dimes, not dollars. Sometimes we overlook activities that don't cost much.

To discover creative new programming ideas, hold a "money meeting" and have kids each bring a dollar bill. Form teams of two or three, and pile the cash in the center of the room. Then let the young people brainstorm creative things they could do as a group with the money in the pile. Have the kids vote for the best activity, then do it. You'll be amazed at how much you can do with so little.

Tap congregational resources. Virtually every church has members who can contribute to your youth ministry in creative ways.

I've found printers who volunteered to produce summer youth event calendars for just the cost of the paper. A TV

Tips for Successful Fund-Raisers

Youth group fund-raisers can be positive or negative experiences. Here are eight ways to make your fund-raisers successful:

1. Be creative. Carwashes can be real washouts, and selling light bulbs can dim your enthusiasm. Think of creative ways to raise funds, like gift wrapping at a local mall during the Christmas season. Or start a penny drive to make the longest line of pennies in the world—with proceeds to the youth program.

2. Make fund-raisers service-oriented. Bake sales are great ideas for fund-raising—unless parents do all the baking. Think of fund-raisers that stretch kids to work for the money. Offer donation-only babysitting services. Hold a "Trash-a-thon" in which kids solicit pledges from church members for every bag of trash they collect during a neighborhood clean-up day.

3. Publicize fund-raisers well. A big carwash won't clean many cars if nobody knows about it. Start publicizing fund-raisers as much as two months in advance. Use fliers, post cards and posters around the neighborhood.

4. Plan fund-raisers well. Throwing together bake sales and carwashes at the last minute usually hurts the church's reputation, the kids' excitement and possible income. It's better to plan one good fund-raiser than five poor ones. As you plan, think about material costs, publicity lead times, personnel needs and other logistics.

5. Get kids involved. Too often adults do all the planning for youth fund-raisers. Have adults and kids work together planning, promoting and participating in the fund-raiser. Everyone will enjoy it more.

6. Limit the number of fund-raisers you sponsor. Holding too many fund-raisers burns out the church, the community and the kids. Try to limit fund-raisers to special events.

7. Keep most fund-raising in the church. Having kids soliciting sales and services from the community can give your church a bad reputation. Fund-raising is best when it takes place in the church, since the money is used to support the church's ministry.

8. Choose fund-raisers carefully. Many Christians dislike church fund-raisers because they seem reminiscent of money-changers in the temple. It's better to raise a smaller amount of money through tasteful fund-raisers than to have your youth group be reprimanded for a poorly chosen scheme.

Budget Savers

You don't have to bust your budget to have creative youth ministry resources. Use these eight ideas for free and low-cost resources.

1. You can get many different youth ministry supplies from local businesses. Consider these:
   - Scratch paper from local printers (in lots of colors!).
   - Newsprint from newspapers, which often throw away paper on the ends of the rolls.
   - Pizza dough from pizza restaurants.
   - Drinks, paper napkins, paper cups and other supplies from fast-food restaurants.
   - Matchbooks from restaurants.
   - Clothes hangers for crafts and activities from dry cleaners.
   - Carpet samples for the youth room floor from carpet suppliers.
   - Appliance boxes from local dealers to create mazes, obstacle courses or even partitions for your meeting area. Also use the stiff cardboard to make publicity signs.

2. Stay up to date on adolescent research by subscribing to Source newsletter. It's free, quarterly, from Search Institute (122 W. Franklin, Ste. 525, Minneapolis, MN 55404), and each issue focuses on a specific adolescent concern.

3. Take your youth group to preview showings of new movies using free promotional tickets. Also contact box offices for music, theater and sports events to see if they have special deals for groups. One youth worker in New York City has taken his low-income kids to Carnegie Hall, Broadway and professional sports events free, using tickets donated by foundations and businesses.

4. Get planning calendars for your youth ministry team from a bank or other business that provides free calendars each year. Before distributing them, highlight important youth ministry dates in each one.

5. The Modern Talking Picture Service (5000 Park St. N., St. Petersburg, FL 33709) has a catalog of free-loan educational films and videos. Combine these resources with Bible study to get your group talking about issues such as health, ecology and technology.

6. Take advantage of free concerts and events in your community. Take the kids to art festivals, outdoor concerts, dramas and other fun, educational—and cheap—activities.

7. Collect two-for-one coupons from local restaurants, then take your kids out for an inexpensive treat.

8. Give your youth group members an inside look at their favorite Christian musicians with the colorful magazine called Premiere. It's free in bundles of 10 from Premiere Services (Box 2120, Chatsworth, CA 91313).

service representative loaned the youth group a television whenever we needed it. And a fast-food restaurant manager volunteered to donate hamburgers for a summer youth group outing. A farmer volunteered his hay and hayrack for a hayride.

Finding people who will share their resources isn't difficult. Just be aware of what people do (professionally and avocationally), then ask when a need arises.

Use resources in your community. Need a film? Many local libraries furnish a good selection. Want a guest speaker? Call your police department and have an officer speak to your group. Need food? Contact local restaurants (especially fast-food) for possible promotions. The "Budget Savers" box on page 107 lists some places to find useful youth group supplies.

Bountiful Resources

Finding adequate resources will always be a challenge in small church youth ministry. Few small churches have the resources to fully fund many different ministries. Thus every program must make sacrifices for the church's good.

Yet all small churches have bountiful resources for youth ministry. Some of those resources are financial. Some are individuals' talents. And some take the form of options that arise when the church uses its creativity to discover programs and ministries that don't rely on big budgets.

Small churches will never match the impressive funding large churches receive—or the impressive programs that result. But, like the wise servants in Jesus' parable (Luke 16:1-9), small churches can learn to wisely use the resources they've been given.

Endnotes

[1] Joani Schultz, "Small Churches and Youth Ministry," GROUP Magazine (February 1985), 67.
[2] Rich Bimler, "Landing a Youth Ministry Budget," GROUP Magazine (October 1982), 18.
[3] Bimler, "Landing a Youth Ministry Budget," 19.

CHAPTER 8

Joining Forces With Other Small Churches

I t's a Friday evening on a warm June day. As the sun slides behind the skyline of the little town, Robert and Jane watch and wait. In minutes, kids from all over town will swarm through the door of the small Presbyterian church for an all-night lock-in.

The youth leaders expect quite a crowd. Not because their little church has such a large youth group. But because the lock-in includes the youth groups from several churches in town.

A year earlier, Robert, Jane and a group of other concerned adults decided it was silly to have youth groups in the small Indiana town competing against each other for programs, resources and kids. So they combined resources, financial bases and creative energy to form one youth group for all the churches. The result has been a stronger youth program for the kids in town as well as a new sense of Christian community and fellowship among the churches.

These Indiana churches joined their whole youth programs. Other small churches maintain distinct youth programs but link with other churches for special activities.

In her book *Youth Ministries: Thinking Big With Small Groups*, Carolyn C. Brown tells about three churches that sponsored a six-week summer program for junior highers. The kids met together once a week for fellowship, Bible study and practice for a youth musical. One church provided a staff music person for the musical, and the other leaders were laypeople from different churches. The pastors alternated leading Bible studies. And 30 kids had an exciting summer experience none of the churches could have sponsored alone.[1]

Benefiting From Cooperative Ministry

These churches represent many churches that have discovered the advantages of networking. They've combined forces and resources with other churches to sponsor youth group events.

Tragically, many small church youth programs compete against each other much more than they cooperate. A town of 1,500 people might have seven churches and five youth groups—all struggling to maintain membership. If they would unite, they could do things not possible with their smaller groups.

Sharing resources—While a small church may not be able to afford expensive videos, curricula, special speakers, publicity or other resources, those things would be within reach for several cooperating churches that contribute financially to a joint program. The churches might even pool their resources to hire a trained youth minister to run the cooperative program. Just think: If eight churches each contributed $300, a cooperative ministry would have a $2,400 budget.

If each church supplied one committed volunteer to the ministry, think of the creative potential! Eight minds together solving problems, discussing programming themes or envisioning goals and dreams.

Networking allows small churches to combine leadership and expertise. A small cadre of volunteers doesn't have to burn itself out planning every youth group activity. Instead, a network would rely on leaders from several churches.

Six churches in a tiny town in upstate New York discovered the value of sharing resources. There were about 100 kids in the local high school, but only one church had a youth group of 10 kids. Four churches didn't have any youth program.

A volunteer youth worker in one church saw the opportunity. He contacted all the churches and convinced them to network. His biggest selling point was that each church would contribute just one adult leader and $15 each month. All the churches agreed.

On the first night of the program, 35 kids showed up. Within six months, the number had jumped to 65 kids! Six of every 10 kids in town was involved. The youth program had become a major focus of community life for teenagers.

Creating enthusiasm—When church youth groups combine for activities, the group instantly grows. The kids—who might not otherwise have many recreation opportunities—can play games and do activities that require more participants.

This interaction adds excitement and enthusiasm to many simulation games, sports and other activities. If apathy comes with low numbers, enthusiasm can be bred through kids coming together for fun and fellowship.

Kids enjoy getting together. A community youth group can be a great force when combined for regular or special programs. Kids get to know other Christian kids, and new friendships develop.

Offering flexibility—Often networks are particularly effective with special events. Churches can plan and lead their own week-to-week activities, but work together to plan special events such as concerts, retreats and camps. They share resources and creativity on big events while keeping their own programs basically intact.

Finding Networking Opportunities

There are dozens of networking opportunities. Here are just a few of the possibilities:

Lock-ins and retreats—Joining with three or four other

churches will allow your retreat or lock-in to be top-notch in every way. Invite a great speaker. Order a film or video. Use the resources of combined forces to create a dynamic and meaningful event.

Fund-raising—Networking automatically creates a work force of many more kids for fund-raising. It also inspires more community support.

Resources—Hundreds of books, films and videos are available for youth ministry. But many cost more than a small church budget can afford. By networking, small churches can have access to more of these resources. The churches agree to purchase particular resources, then each church has access to them. This same system can also be used to purchase equipment such as videocassette recorders or photocopiers.

Be sure to organize your resource network. You might form a central library and have individual churches pay monthly or annual fees, which are used to buy new resources. Or simply have each church submit a list of the resources it owns. Then combine the lists so churches know where to borrow particular resources.

Service projects—Have youth groups band together to work in the community. Scrub graffiti off walls. Pick up trash along an interstate. Clean store windows. By working together, several groups can accomplish much bigger projects.

Youth leadership training—A group of Florida churches has held successful annual youth ministry training events. Because of their cooperation, they can afford to bring in noted youth ministry experts. One year, more than 200 people attended the training event. The total membership of all seven churches was barely twice that number.

Parent support—Churches can network to provide excellent parent forums on topics ranging from adolescent development to youth gangs. Churches can also provide family events. Or they can start a parenting newsletter.

Special events—Dozens of special events become possible through networking. Go skiing at a nearby resort. Host New Year's Eve parties. Sponsor Christian roller-skating nights. Plan tours to Christian colleges. The possibilities are endless.

Understanding the Fears

If networking works so well, why don't more small churches do it? A primary reason is fear.

Fear that kids will "church hop"—What if you joined with other youth groups in your community, and kids in your group discovered they liked another church better? You could lose all your kids.

This is a common fear, particularly if a group is small. You may feel sheltering kids from other churches will keep them from leaving your program. In reality, sheltering rarely works— at least not for long. If your church isn't meeting kids' needs, they'll move on. And they'll hear about other programs from friends at school.

Fear that kids will drop out—Some churches worry that networking will prompt some kids to drop out of church completely because they enjoyed being part of a small group. In the larger group, these kids might feel lost in the crowd. Yet this fear rarely comes true. Kids enjoy the large group as well. And the problem is overcome entirely by alternating between large and small group activities

Fear of losing control—If we networked, people say, kids would spend time in other churches. We wouldn't always choose what they studied or did. We wouldn't have control over the youth program.

Controlling churches will have difficulty networking. By definition, cooperation involves give-and-take. A single church can't govern all aspects of the program. So kids might do things differently when another church leads. They might sing different songs, use different learning techniques, experience different emphases.

These differences may seem negative on the surface. But they're actually positive, because they help kids appreciate and work with people who are different from them.

Fear that beliefs will be compromised—"Who knows what they'll teach our kids at that other church!" cries a leader who resists networking. Some people fear their kids will be "stained" by false doctrines at another church.

This fear is a central concern, particularly in interdenominational networking. The following section suggests specific ways to deal with the issue.

Overcoming Potential Problems

Most fears and problems can be overcome with careful planning and mutual understanding. Here are some guidelines and suggestions.

Handling differences—Whenever churches with traditions, emphases and expressions work together, there will be disagreements. They may involve doctrinal issues. They may involve worship style—songs, prayers, liturgy or other practices (such as baptism or communion). Or differences may arise over youth ministry emphases. One church might emphasize fellowship, another might push evangelism and discipleship, and another might focus on Christian service.

These differences are inevitable. But the differences don't have to prevent cooperation. Overcome the problem in the following ways:

• Love—This is what cooperative effort is all about, right? Love for the kids. Love for brothers and sisters in Christ. Love puts differences in perspective.

• Communication—This is a natural result of love. By talking about differences and needs, you'll discover creative ways to solve the problem. Pre-empt potential problems by keeping each church informed about plans, including upcoming topics and emphases.

• Focus—Develop a purpose statement for the ministry. Why do you want the cooperative ministry? What is its purpose? By focusing on the reason for being, other elements become less divisive.

Begin by developing a purpose statement. If disagreements arise, refer to the purpose statement in light of the problem. If the disputed concern isn't important to your purpose, maybe you should drop it. But if it's vital, talk about it—in love—and develop a creative solution.

• Flexibility—Being flexible is a key to working together.

Suppose, for example, doctrinal differences have become a major concern in your network. Think of creative solutions.

You may decide to share in social and service activities, but to have each congregation lead its own Bible study and discipleship. In this way, churches can each maintain their unique faith perspective while still interacting with other churches.

Another option would be to break into church groups when discussing controversial areas—with an adult from each church facilitating the discussion.

• Openness—Differences can often become rich learning experiences. By being open to differing views, we often learn more about ourselves and our faith. Conflict doesn't have to be negative, it can be an opportunity to grow.

Many churches find the experiences in other churches enriching rather than threatening. As young people experience other expressions of Christ's body, their experience broadens and their faith deepens.

Arranging logistics—Logistics can become another source of friction when churches network. Where should the group meet? Who should lead? Who should manage the budget?

There are two basic ways to address this potential problem:

• Keep everything neutral. Don't meet in anyone's church; meet in a community center or a school gymnasium instead. (Many small churches don't have facilities for a large cooperative youth program anyway.) Hire or choose a leader without strong ties to any individual congregation. In this way, no church will be perceived as more important.

• Rotate among churches. A second option is to share leadership and facilities among cooperating churches. For example, each month you could hold meetings at the Baptist church one week, the Methodist church the next, the Lutheran church the next and the independent church the last week. Use a similar rotation pattern for planning, leadership and volunteers.

In this way, each church has responsibility for the whole

group on a regular basis. And the individual groups can learn from and about each other through the month.

Dealing with jealousy—When a new kid joins the cooperative youth group, which church does he or she belong to?

Such a controversy nearly ripped apart a youth ministry network in California. The network pooled resources to sponsor big events such as Christian concerts. The program worked well until people discovered a few of the churches were reaping more harvest than everyone else! One youth group had added to its rolls nearly 45 percent of the respondents at a recent evangelistic crusade.

This caused quite a fury. Several churches pulled out of the network altogether. Why should they contribute time and money to a network that did little good for their program?

When such questions arise, keep these two priorities in mind. First, a teenager should be allowed to choose which congregation he or she wants to affiliate with. Second, the purpose of cooperation is to build the body of Christ, not necessarily to build each congregation. Congregations should celebrate when a young person becomes active in a church instead of muttering that he or she chose a different congregation.

Sharing the load—A key reason for doing cooperative youth ministry events is to share the work. But sometimes one or two churches find themselves doing all the work. Or one particularly gifted volunteer ends up doing counseling for all the churches. So the cooperative effort doesn't ease the load but increases it—without adding resources or support.

This potential danger is an important reason for spelling out responsibilities in writing early in your cooperative venture. Then churches and individuals should hold each other accountable for maintaining their commitments—and for not rescuing other churches that don't do their part. Unless everyone maintains commitment, the cooperation will fizzle.

Handling cliques—A potential danger in a cooperative ministry is that kids from each church form cliques. Their friends from church will often be the people they want to be with.

But this tendency can be overcome with proper programming and effective crowdbreakers. Build a sense of community and camaraderie within the cooperative group. As kids interact, they'll gradually develop new friendships. However, if cliques persist beyond six months or so, leaders should evaluate the problem and decide how to overcome it.

Designing Cooperative Programs

How do you get a youth ministry network started in your community? Use the following plan to pull together a youth ministry network:

Step 1—Write a letter inviting youth leaders from churches in your community to an initial "dream meeting." Explain your vision and your initial ideas.

Step 2—Host the meeting. Spend time getting to know each other. Discuss your idea, and list all pros and cons. Have people brainstorm various programs you might cooperate in. Then develop a consensus on the approach to propose to the congregations.

Step 3—Have youth leaders from each congregation take the idea to their congregations. Encourage them to solicit ideas as well as concerns.

Step 4—Bring together people from all the churches that expressed interest in the networking idea. Address concerns that were raised in congregations. Discuss in more detail the options, and begin narrowing the best approach for your situation. (You may, for example, need to try a few special events before launching into full-fledged cooperative ministry.)

Once you've agreed on an approach, write a preliminary mission statement for the network. Include the purpose as well as the approach. For example, you might decide to sponsor only four joint events each year. Or you might conclude that your churches should unite programs completely.

Also, develop a more detailed proposal that outlines each church's responsibilities. Include finances, leadership, facilities and other commitments you're asking the congregations to make.

Have youth leaders take the proposal to their congregations for feedback, additional ideas and approval. Set a target date for having a final, approved plan.

Step 5—Once churches have accepted the mission statement, develop a coordinating committee for the program. Include people from every congregation. Make sure some people on the committee are teenagers. Divide responsibilities according to the specific approach you've chosen.

Step 6—Plan a kickoff event to introduce your cooperative youth program. Publicize it widely in all the churches. Include all the congregations so church members will understand the idea and support the ministry. Contact local newspapers—the novel ministry is sure to attract interest!

Step 7—Use your kickoff event to build momentum, then keep it going. Continue to publicize your events to build enthusiasm and keep kids interested. Spend lots of time on group-building in early sessions. Help kids build relationships and get comfortable interacting.

Step 8—Maintain regular contact with each congregation. Encourage leaders from the different churches to write articles about the ministry for their own church newsletters. Ask for regular feedback from the congregations to determine what's being accepted and what isn't. Adjust the program as needed.

Step 9—Evaluate at regular intervals. Your initial proposal may need to be changed once your program is going. At first, have evaluation sessions after every meeting or event. Later, evaluate every six months. Ask group members for their opinions and ideas.

As you continue to evaluate and adjust, your program will become stronger. And your ministry will be more effective in meeting kids' needs.

Remembering the Possibilities

When an Amish family needs a house, the community has a house-raising. In one day—from dawn to dusk—community members build the whole house. Something that usually takes months is completed in hours. People set aside their individual jobs for the day to work together to build the house.

Amish cooperation illustrates what's possible through networking. We see people working together for a common goal. For the house-raising, the goal is building a home. For youth ministry, it's helping young people grow in Christ. We also see people sharing their gifts and abilities so others can benefit.

Networking may mean forfeiting personal biases and preferences. It may mean humility rather than pride. But God honors such mutual submission.

Maybe that's why networking works.

Endnotes

1 Carolyn C. Brown, *Youth Ministries: Thinking Big With Small Groups* (Nashville, TN: Abingdon Press, 1984), 54.

CHAPTER 9

But What About Me?

"**H**elp! Help!"

The young mother's screams shattered the salty sea air.

"My daughter fell overboard!" she cried, frantically looking for anyone to help.

Within seconds an old man was swimming through the ocean waves toward the outstretched hand of the little girl. She clasped her tiny arms about his neck, and the old man swam back to the luxury liner with the girl safely in tow.

A hero! The old man had bravely risked his life.

That night, the man sat at the captain's table as a guest of honor. Following the meal, the captain stood and asked the packed dining room for silence as he paid tribute to the hero. The crowd listened in awe as the captain told of the courageous rescue. Following his inspiring speech, the captain asked the old man to share a few words about his daring display of courage.

First there was a standing ovation. Then silent anticipation and admiration as the old man took the microphone. He hadn't spoken to anyone all day about his unselfish act. The old man surveyed the packed room and gave what must have been the shortest hero speech in history.

"All right," he finally said. "I just want to know who pushed me in."

• • •

It's easy to feel like that old man when you do youth ministry in a small church. After long hours of preparation, heart-to-heart talks and narrow escapes from lock-in shaving cream fights, you may ask, "All right, who pushed me in?"

Why do you do it? How do you stay motivated?

What are your personal concerns? How do you effectively manage your time? How do you measure your success?

Take this quiz to evaluate the personal side of your ministry. Check the box that best represents your initial reaction.

1. It's Saturday night, and I still haven't prepared to teach Sunday school. So I . . .
   ☐ assume no one will show up anyway and don't worry about it.
   ☐ realize I can teach a decent lesson if I start studying now.
   ☐ turn on the television, and plan to "wing it."
   ☐ start preparing, but commit myself to doing better next week.
2. I think of my daily calendar as . . .
   ☐ good liner for my bird cage.
   ☐ something that makes me look busy.
   ☐ something to doodle in during sermons and committee meetings.
   ☐ a useful tool to keep me organized and efficient.
3. I see other youth leaders in the church as . . .
   ☐ good people to blow up balloons and paint props.
   ☐ people who do things I don't like to do.
   ☐ unneeded baggage. I can run the show by myself.
   ☐ partners in ministry to guide and train as they share responsibilities.
4. On my day off, I usually . . .
   ☐ visit youth group members and potential new members.
   ☐ prepare for the next youth group meeting.
   ☐ What day off?
   ☐ relax.

5. When I get together with other youth leaders for lunch, we . . .
   - ☐ draw caricatures of our pastors.
   - ☐ complain about church members who make our jobs difficult.
   - ☐ share the latest gossip and down burgers.
   - ☐ support one another through encouragement and prayer.
6. Small church youth ministry success is . . .
   - ☐ becoming (or moving to) a big church.
   - ☐ having a youth group of 50 singing "Kum Ba Yah" in a prayer circle.
   - ☐ having kids chant my name when I walk into a room.
   - ☐ seeing kids become mature Christian leaders.
7. Continuing education is for . . .
   - ☐ people who want a sheepskin to hang in the office.
   - ☐ senior pastors.
   - ☐ youth ministers who can't find a job in a church.
   - ☐ any youth leader who wants to sharpen skills.

If you checked any squares but the last one on each question, it's time to re-evaluate your priorities and motives. You may be having trouble with burnout and frustration. This chapter gives you tools to help you survive—and thrive—as a small church youth leader. It discusses:

- time management;
- support networks;
- perspective;
- personal growth; and
- spiritual nourishment.

Time Management

Thomas Mann once wrote, "Hold fast the time. Guard it, watch over it, every hour, every minute, unguarded it slips away, like a lizard, smooth, slippery, faithless. Hold every minute sacred."[1]

If any single issue dominates the concerns of youth leaders

in small churches, it's time. There always seems to be more to do than there is time for. And if we don't learn to control the problem, we burn out. In fact, a survey of youth workers found the #1 reason they would consider leaving their ministry positions is burnout.[2]

That's why learning to manage time well is so important. Here are some hints:

Set limits. In his book *Getting a Grip on Time Management*, Les Christie compares youth workers to Shukuni Sasaki, a Japanese plate spinner who holds the world record of twirling 72 plates at the same time. As youth workers, Christie writes, we often operate our programs like twirling plates on large poles.[3] We get one program rolling, then start another one. Now we have two. Seeing another need, we spin a third program.

Before long, the first program slows down, so we go back and give it another twirl. Then we start a fourth program. And a fifth (but only after making two and three spin just a little harder). Pretty soon, we are doing nothing but keeping the programs running. And without our occasional spins, they would come crashing down.

The problem can be particularly difficult in small churches, because of the temptation to try to create elaborate, multifaceted programs like we see in larger churches. As youth workers, we have to determine how many plates we can juggle without having some crash. Use the "Am I Doing Too Much?" worksheet on page 124 to evaluate your youth ministry workload.

Plan ahead. One characteristic of small churches is they often don't plan ahead. They don't have to deal with large-church bureaucracy, so they wait until the last minute to do anything.

That was Paul's experience when he joined a small church youth ministry leadership team. Each month the group would meet to figure out what was happening that month. And every time, events would creep up unexpected. So—usually two weeks before the planned event—Paul would be asked to send out publicity or order resources.

Am I Doing Too Much?

Instructions: Are you trying to do too much in your ministry? Use the following steps to evaluate your workload.

1. How many young people are in your church's youth program? _____

2. List the church programs you currently have responsibility for:

3. List any programs you'd like to see developed in the coming year:

4. Go back to step 3 and circle all the programs you believe require your guidance to get started.

5. Next to each program in steps 2 and 3, name someone in your church who could handle the responsibility. (Include the programs you circled.)

6. List other responsibilities you have (other jobs, school, family responsibilities) and how much time you spend on them each week:

Responsibility	**Time Spent**

7. List hobbies, exercise, relaxation and other personal interests and how much time you'd realistically like to spend on them each week:

Interest	**Time Needed**

continued

8. Using steps 2, 3, 6 and 7 as starting points, schedule an ideal week. Give yourself a day off too.

Week of _____	Monday	Tuesday	Wednesday	Thursday	Friday	Saturday	Sunday
Morning							
Afternoon							
Evening							

9. Evaluate your situation. Considering the number of teenagers you work with, the time you spend on responsibilities and programs, mark where you feel you are on the following continuum:

_____

   1 2 3   4   5   6   7   8   9   10

There's no way   I've got time

I could survive   to burn.

such a week.

10. Now evaluate your score:
- •9-10: You have some time to develop new programs. Go to your list in step 3 and make your dreams come true.
- •7-8: You have some extra time. Select one program from step 3 to put into action this year.
- •5-6: You're maintaining a sizable load, but it seems balanced. Make wise choices about what you'll do and what you'll turn down so your score doesn't decrease.
- •3-4: You're under pressure. Don't take on any more responsibilities. Look for ways to ease your load by passing a program or responsibility to someone else.
- •1-2: Take emergency action. You won't last long with this kind of load. Start calling the people you listed in step 5 to take over some of your responsibilities. Or let a program die. And practice saying "No. No. No."

Of course, people always said, "We've got to plan ahead next time." But they never did.

Planning not only makes your ministry stronger, but it also saves time. When things are planned, you don't spend as much time frantically gathering all the pieces you need. Also, when you plan, you can often piggyback jobs. For example, you can order resources for several months instead of scrambling to find resources for a particular retreat. And you can save valuable church resources because you have more time to look for bargains.

Susan is a youth leader in a small Minnesota church. When she has a big event planned, she lists all the jobs to be accomplished and then backdates her calendar in order to get everything done. You won't find Susan ordering a film two weeks before a lock-in. She tries to have most major tasks done at least two weeks ahead of the event. That way, she can be flexible if something unexpected pops up.

Personal planning is also helpful in saving time. List all scheduled events and activities on a daily calendar. Add reminders of when to start planning and publicizing particular events. And block out time for yourself and your family.

Delegate, delegate, delegate. When Joanne's church asks her to lead a program, you can be sure she'll do it—all of it. Since the group is small, she says she doesn't need any help. She'll find the resources, develop the idea, create the publicity, make the announcements, prepare the refreshments, sing the special music, lead the prayer—and collapse after the meeting. She won't be able to do anything else in the church for months.

Joanne needs to learn what many leaders need to learn: how to delegate. One of the main reasons small church youth workers burn out is because they never give other people responsibilities.

The key to delegating is to learn what *you* need to do and what *others* can do. For every task, ask yourself, "Am I the best person to do this, or can someone else take this responsibility?" Why should you struggle for hours to design publicity when another youth leader or youth group member has an artistic knack and loves putting together fliers? All you have to do is ask.

Delegation can be particularly difficult in a small church. Everyone is already busy with other responsibilities. And some youth leaders feel guilty delegating, because they feel the youth work is their responsibility. But delegation is an important way to share your ministry. Here are some ideas to make it work in a small church:

• Give small assignments. Instead of delegating all the work for an upcoming fund-raiser to one person, assign publicity to one, supplies to another, worker coordination to another and money collection to another.

• If someone says no once, don't assume that he or she isn't interested in helping. Find out when that person can serve and what he or she would like to do. Keep the information handy, then ask again.

• For bigger tasks, assign two people to work together. They can divide responsibilities, encourage each other and build a strong relationship.

• When you give someone a job, also give them authority to make decisions within guidelines you agree upon. You won't be bothered by constant requests for permission. And the person will feel more fulfilled in carrying out the responsibility. The person may not do it exactly as you would do it, but his or her approach could be just as effective.

Rest. A final element of time management is to give yourself a break. Regularly take a day off.

It sounds contradictory, doesn't it? But it's not. Rest is a key to using your time well. In his book *Beating Burnout in Youth Ministry*, Dean Feldmeyer describes the tendency youth workers have to work incessantly:

> When I started doing things more efficiently, I was sometimes tempted to fill the free time I'd created with more tasks. After all, that's what people expect from youth workers. So I'd say to myself: "Gee, it only takes half the usual time to answer the mail. Maybe I'll develop a brand-new Bible study

for tonight's meeting. That'd be much better than modifying an old one, wouldn't it?"

But adding more tasks to fill your time only adds to the stress and burnout. If you're like most dedicated youth workers, you already do enough. So use the time you've made to take care of yourself and your family.[4]

The first way to rest is to take a day off each week—faithfully. Some professional youth leaders take off a weekday because Saturdays are often spent on youth group activities.

If you're a volunteer youth leader, you may have more trouble getting time off. Sure, your regular job may give you a two-day weekend, but how do you spend those two days? With the kids, in a committee or in preparation for your next Bible study or meeting? So it's even more important not to become overcommitted to the youth group. If you need a break or rest, tell someone. Let other people handle some of the responsibilities.

It's also important to carve out time for your family. Monday and Thursday evenings are my family times. Only an occasional church meeting on Monday night will change that schedule. I do nothing else on those nights but spend time with my wife and daughter.

The hardest word in the world to say is also one of the smallest. It only has two letters: n and o. No. If you have trouble saying it, practice in front of the mirror each morning. Then use it when you start feeling pressured.

Support Networks

Many small church youth workers pretend they're indestructible. They don't need other people's support. They can solve their own problems.

But they're wrong. Human beings are social creatures. We need each other. We need to share with people who understand our struggles, our victories, our dreams and our needs. We need people who will support us and nourish us so we have the stamina and inner resources to continue in our ministries. We need a support network. That needed support can take many forms.

• Get together with other youth workers in your area. Share your joys, struggles, questions and stories. Support, encourage and pray for one another.

Check around your area to see if such a group already meets. If you can't find an existing group, start one. Contact nearby youth workers in small churches and explain your interest. Chances are good they feel the same need. Together you can support each other in the unique concerns you have in your small churches.

• Develop spiritual accountability with a trusted friend— someone who will encourage and listen to you, and challenge and even rebuke you. It can be a church member, a youth worker in another church or a trusted friend.

• Support each other on the youth ministry or Christian education team. When you meet, don't spend all your time planning. Spend time praying and sharing concerns. Get together away from the youth group. Do some fun things together. Build a relationship so you know you can always turn to each other for support and encouragement.

Perspective

Bob is a great lay youth leader. He has worked in his 70-member country church for more than eight years. His youth group is nothing unusual. He's lucky if 10 kids come to meetings.

The only thing that's frustrating to Bob is that other people don't see his ministry as successful. Every year Bob attends an all-day youth ministry training seminar in a nearby city (he takes a vacation day to do it). He sits in seminars featuring youth ministry experts from around the country telling about their successes. They boast of programs with hundreds of kids. They talk of huge youth budgets. They describe flashy publicity and zany programming ideas.

And every year Bob leaves the event disappointed. What

should be a time of encouragement, growth and new ideas often makes Bob feel like a youth ministry failure.

All around you people imply—or say outright—that success in youth ministry is in numbers. Or ministering in a large church. Or receiving recognition from peers. And those things rarely happen in small churches.

Lyle Schaller illustrates the problem well in *The Small Church Is Different!* In many denominations, he writes, "the unofficial, or informal, policy begins to question the competence, the ambition, or the responsiveness of the minister who has been serving the same small-membership church for ten consecutive years."[5]

So how do you cope with the lack of status given to small church youth ministry? Here are three suggestions:

• First, remember your priorities. You're not in ministry for status. You're in ministry to touch kids' lives. If that statement doesn't seem true to you, evaluate your motives.

• Second, find other measurements. Don't measure your success by numbers and status and recognition. Measure it by the little changes you see in your kids' lives. Focus on your ministry's impact instead of its volume.

• Finally, give God your ministry. In an age where success is measured by name and accomplishments, God blesses small church youth workers for their faithfulness. Maturity and faith bring peace. Jesus didn't call us to be successful, he called us to be faithful.

Personal Growth

Youth ministry is becoming more specialized as the problems our teenagers face become more complex and troubling. Even small churches have group members from dysfunctional families and kids with special problems. In fact, since small churches often attract kids who are "outcasts" in society, you may deal with a disproportionate share of troubled kids.

For volunteer youth leaders these issues can be particularly challenging. Volunteers rarely have the training, or experience to feel comfortable addressing tough needs.

To address these concerns and to maintain your vitality, interest and skills, find opportunities for continuing education. There are many valuable approaches to continuing education, both formal and informal.

Advanced degrees—Professional youth workers reap significant benefits from the discipline of an advanced degree. A bachelor's degree lays a foundation for ministry. Advanced degrees give you opportunities to explore particular skills and areas of expertise such as counseling, biblical studies or family ministry.

Workshops and seminars—Many national organizations and denominations sponsor training events for youth workers. Some last several days; some are one-day workshops. These events—which are open to professionals and laypeople— expose you to numerous ministry ideas as well as the latest resources. Moreover, they provide an atmosphere of support and worship. While some workshops are expensive, you can often find bargains in your area if you look.

You may also find inexpensive and valuable workshops and classes available through local community colleges and organizations. These might include classes in adolescent development, time and stress management, leadership, drama or dozens of other topics. Take advantage of the opportunities, then adapt the information to your youth ministry situation.

Reading—Reading is a flexible and inexpensive way to improve your youth ministry knowledge. Christian publishers produce hundreds of books that address virtually every aspect of youth ministry. Read those that address your situation and needs. Set personal goals for regular reading. Subscribe to a youth ministry periodical such as GROUP Magazine (see resource listing on page 164). Each month you'll find new ideas for your ministry.

Networking—Don't rely on your own experience for all your ideas. Talk to other youth leaders in small churches. Visit their congregations. Exchange newsletters. Find out what problems they're encountering and how they're dealing with them. Look for ideas you can use in your ministry. It won't cost much, and the benefits can be tremendous.

Spiritual Nourishment

It's a sad statistic. According to a survey by Dr. Mark Lamport of Gordon College, 48 percent of youth workers feel spiritually empty.[6]

I can relate.

This past summer my spiritual well was drawn upon time and time again for camp programs, youth trips and sermons. As my time got tighter, I allowed my daily fellowship with God to be squeezed out. In fact, I went for several months without cracking the Bible for a personal drink.

And I dried up.

Since then I've made my spiritual walk a central priority in my day. Oh, I still fall. I still mess up. But God is working.

Keeping God first is never easy in small church youth ministry. Something will always be there to crowd out your daily time with God. Keep your focus with these ideas:

Make quiet time a priority. I love to eat. I love to eat so much I rarely miss a meal. First thing every morning, I hop out of bed and head for the pantry to satisfy my breakfast habit. I couldn't get through the day without eating. Hamburgers. Pizzas. Steak and corn. Lasagna. My mouth is already watering!

I also love God. Yet, when I look back at my daily meals with him, I'm malnourished. Missing a spiritual meal isn't bad, I tell myself. I can stay fit and trim. But as the demands of ministry pile on each other, that single meal turns into several missed meals. Days become weeks. Weeks become months.

To keep that from happening, find one hour every day that's automatically God's time. It doesn't have to be formal. In fact, if you commute to work, you can listen to the Bible on tape and pray (eyes open, of course!) while you're driving. Or do Bible study as you ride the stationary bicycle.

Make quiet time quiet. Daily quiet times can be just about anywhere. In the hallway closet. In a car. In the church basement. On a park bench. By a lake. But it needs to be fairly quiet and free of disruptions.

That can be difficult in a small church. I used to have quiet times in my office. However, a flashing phone line, a knock on the door or a pile of work on my desk often cut my time short. So now I get away from the office where I can be by myself.

Explain to other people (your family, other youth leaders, group members) your need for privacy. If they want to visit, say, "I really do want to visit with you, but I need to spend time alone right now. Can we talk in an hour?"

Make quiet time creative. Spending time with God is far from boring. If it seems boring to you, make it creative.

Take prayer, for example. Too often it becomes a meaningless routine. But prayer can be done many different ways. Instead of kneeling, lie flat on your back. Instead of closing your eyes, open them and take a walk through the church neighborhood praising God for his work there.

You can also have a personal worship service. Use relaxing Christian recordings. Allow each song to guide you through thanksgiving and petition. Make up your own praise songs. If you enjoy poetry, write your thoughts in verse and rhyme.

● ● ●

Small church youth ministry demands spiritual depth. When the wellspring of life is dry and you're pumping only air, your message is as parched and empty as the wind. Such a spiritual desert may not only be fatal to you, it may also be deadly to your kids. So dig your well deep.

The water inside can quench a thirsty world.

Endnotes

[1] Quoted in Les Christie, *Getting a Grip on Time Management* (Wheaton, IL: Victor Books, 1984), 5.

[2] Eugene C. Roehlkepartain, *The Youth Ministry Resource Book* (Loveland, CO: Group Books, 1988), 189.

[3] Christie, *Getting a Grip on Time Management,* 7.

[4] Dean Feldmeyer, *Beating Burnout in Youth Ministry* (Loveland, CO: Group Books, 1989), 110.

[5] Lyle Schaller, *The Small Church Is Different!* (Nashville, TN: Abingdon Press, 1982), 14.

[6] Roehlkepartain, *The Youth Ministry Resource Book,* 187.

CHAPTER 10

Different Ministries, Different Needs

S usan leads the youth ministry program at her 100-member suburban church in northern California. She has no formal youth ministry training, she's never attended a youth ministry class, and she rarely has time to read youth ministry books or periodicals. The only resources she has are the ones in the church library—and it doesn't have a good collection.

Yet Susan is in charge of all activities, curriculum needs and service projects for her church's junior and senior high groups. Susan's the first to admit such responsibilities often leave her exhausted. But she keeps doing it because she loves the kids.

• • •

If you ask Kurt about his church's youth ministry, he'll groan. As the pastor of a small suburban church, Kurt struggles to maintain all the ministries in the congregation. He enjoys most of them—particularly the ones that involve young adults. But the youth ministry is no fun for him—and hasn't been for years. He has trouble relating to kids, and he's lost interest in all the topics young people want to talk about.

But he keeps plugging along, trying to keep the youth program strong. He knows it's important for attracting new families, and he believes in providing ministries for people of all ages. Kurt knows pastors who really enjoy working with kids. But it's a tedious struggle for Kurt.

• • •

Phil has just finished another week of seminary classes. While his friends head for weekends of concerts, movies and socials, Phil heads toward a small church in a southern Illinois town. He's the church's part-time youth minister.

Over the weekend, Phil will attend a high school basketball game, meet several group members for a prayer breakfast, design a flier for an upcoming activity and counsel with a mother. He will also visit a couple of group members, take the junior highers to the park, teach Sunday school, lead the youth group meeting and help with the morning worship service.

• • •

Carla is a full-time youth worker in inner-city Omaha. She does full-time work, but hardly gets full-time pay. She sometimes takes odd jobs so she can afford to continue in ministry. As part of her ministry, she spends a lot of time as a counselor in a nearby high school and also volunteers at the YMCA.

Carla regularly gets offers from large churches to be their youth minister. But she stays in the small church because she's dedicated to her kids.

• • •

Susan, Kurt, Phil and Carla are committed to helping teenagers. But each is involved in youth ministry in a different way. As a result, each has different frustrations and needs. And each represents one of the four types of small church youth workers:

- the volunteer youth worker;
- the pastor with youth ministry responsibilities;
- the part-time youth worker; and
- the full-time youth worker.

The Volunteer Youth Worker

Volunteers with little or no youth ministry training run most small church youth ministry programs. The congregations often don't have resources to hire professionals. Some don't even have full-time pastors.

Other congregations have so few young people they can't justify hiring a youth minister. They choose to emphasize other ministries, or they assign youth ministry as one of many responsibilities in an assistant pastor's job description.

Volunteer youth workers in small churches have tremendous ministry opportunities. As Joani Schultz writes to volunteers, "In a sense, you're free to do your best without the high expectations often dumped on a paid professional . . . Church members see you as one of them; they can be more understanding, supportive, and forgiving."[1]

Also, volunteers can often build stronger relationships with teenagers than paid staff can. Kids know that volunteers participate because they want to—not because they're paid to.

Terry and Roxie Allen are typical volunteers. They lead the youth ministry program at a small church in Ft. Benton, Montana—a town of 1,500 with seven churches.

The Allens started working with the youth group three years ago. In addition to regular meetings, the Allens invite kids to their ranch and lead an annual backpack trip into Glacier National Park. Under their leadership, the youth group has grown stronger and larger.

Volunteers' frustrations—Even in light of their successful ministry, Terry and Roxie feel the frustrations common to volunteers who lead youth ministries.

- Lack of time with young people—In addition to their full-time jobs, Terry and Roxie spend 10 to 15 hours each week with the youth group. But Terry confesses, "There's just not enough time to do everything. There's only so much we can do."

• Lack of personal time—When volunteer youth leaders work all week in another job and spend several evenings and every weekend at the church, they're left with little time for themselves, their families or other outside interests. While professional youth workers often get a day off, volunteers tend to spend their two "days off" working at the church.

• Lack of training—Without training, many volunteers feel inadequate in youth ministry. If a program doesn't work, they struggle to find the problem. If a teenager reports trouble at home, they're not sure how to respond. If the church doesn't support the ministry, they don't know how to build the support. They feel like parents caught assembling toys on Christmas Eve without instructions.

• Lack of resources—It's hard to know what youth ministry resources will work for your group. And even when a volunteer does find useful resources, money is still tight.

A side effect of this problem is that volunteer youth leaders have trouble staying motivated and keeping current. On the isolated plains of north-central Montana, the Allens realize keeping current will always be difficult.

• Lack of congregational support—Some volunteer leaders feel they've been abandoned in the youth ministry program. No one will help with the ministry (everyone else has several responsibilities in the church). And certainly no one is ready to take over the youth ministry.

So they feel trapped. If they stay in their job, they're prime candidates for burnout and apathy. If they leave, they feel oppressive guilt, especially if no one takes over.

• Lack of communication with church staff and leaders— Small church pastors, staff people and other church leaders have hectic lives in small churches. When they find good volunteers to lead a particular program, they often turn over all responsibilities, sigh with relief and forget about that ministry.

On the other hand, sometimes the volunteer who takes charge of the program wants total control of the youth ministry. The less "interference" from the church staff, the better.

In either case, the result is the same: lack of communication. Little communication may seem okay—until a problem comes along. Then suddenly the volunteer feels isolated, unappreciated and without support. Or if the problem results because of the volunteer's leadership approach, church leaders find themselves in a difficult situation demanding some sort of confrontation.

Volunteer survival—Volunteer youth ministry *can* be successful and rewarding. Here are some suggestions for overcoming the frustrations:

• Get training. Training overcomes many frustrations of volunteer youth ministry. Not only do you learn new skills to be more effective and efficient in your ministry, but the training stimulates your creativity and interest. And when training involves interaction with other youth leaders, their ideas, stories and affirmation invigorate your own ministry.

Training can take many forms. Invite a local youth minister to come speak in your church. Secure a training video and conduct a training series. Order audio tapes. Subscribe to youth ministry magazines. Read books. Attend area seminars or national youth ministry training and inspiration events.

Ask the church to include money for training in the youth ministry budget. The Allens' church helps pay their way to an annual youth leaders convention in the Midwest. The event helps the Allens stay motivated and current while teaching them new skills.

• Set realistic limits. The only way to survive in volunteer youth ministry is to set limits. You can't run a huge program with multiple programming options. You can't meet every kid's need. You can't spend every spare hour in youth ministry. You can't do everything. And if you try, you'll become even more frustrated and burned out.

Set limits on the number of evenings you'll spend at church each week. Limit the number of Saturdays and Sunday afternoons you'll devote to church activities. Then make choices.

If you decide to spend no more than two evenings at the church, and someone schedules a meeting for a third evening, say you can't make it. If you can't do everything in the amount of time you set, find someone else to help—or cancel the program. This may sound harsh, but it's the only way to maintain your sanity.

To evaluate your own schedule, use the "Am I Doing Too Much?" worksheet on page 124 in Chapter 9.

• Schedule creatively. One way to find more time for your ministry is through creative scheduling. Instead of always fighting your schedule, find ways to make the schedule work for you.

If you need to spend more time with kids, think of informal ways to get together with several kids at the same time. The Allens try to attend Friday night ball games with youth group members. Sometimes they invite kids over to their house just for fun.

Another way to save time is to schedule activities in clumps. If, for example, you have a church meeting at 6 p.m. on Wednesday, plan your touch-base meeting with the pastor at 5:30—maybe over a light dinner. By scheduling several meetings in a single evening, you keep other evenings free. You also eliminate wasted travel time.

• Communicate with everyone. Regular communication is vital in volunteer youth ministry. Communicate with kids. Communicate with parents. Communicate with the pastor. Communicate with committees, boards and other church leaders.

Meet regularly with your pastor. Coordinate your programs with church programs. Make sure your planning and leadership is on track and consistent with the church's mission. Learn from others' experience and leadership. Turn to them with questions, and seek their advice when you're confronted with a problem you don't feel prepared to handle.

Also share your dreams, frustrations, successes, problems and needs with other church leaders. When they understand your ministry, they'll support and encourage you. Clear every activity, curriculum and program through the appropriate channels. It may sound tedious and unnecessary, but it prevents misunderstanding later on.

• Limit commitment. As a volunteer leader, it's important you wholeheartedly commit yourself to the assignment. But that's hard to do if the assignment feels like a life sentence.

Encourage your church to develop a job description for your position (see page 90 for a sample). Include a two-year limit (or shorter) on the commitment. You may decide to continue beyond that, but it should be clear you have fulfilled your commitment at that time.

• Take breaks. If possible, take "vacations" from youth ministry during the year. December and January are great months to call Youth Worker Months Off. Another option is to meet only four weekends each month. If a month has five weekends, take a break.

• Share the ministry. No one should be asked to lead a youth ministry alone. If youth ministry is important to the congregation, other people will support the program. Ask for help. Chapter 6 deals with finding volunteers in the small church.

The Pastor With Youth Ministry Responsibilities

Most small church pastors are the church's only staff member, so the pastor inevitably is responsible for overseeing all areas of the church's ministry—including the youth ministry.

For some pastors, youth ministry is an enjoyable outlet. Susan, for example, served as a youth minister in a large church for several years before becoming the "solo" pastor of a small church. While her concern and ministry have broadened to include the rest of the congregation, she still enjoys working directly with young people.

On the other hand, Dan has never worked in youth ministry. He feels awkward and uncomfortable around kids. To make matters worse, he hears rumors that youth group members think he's too aloof and boring. For Dan, youth ministry is the albatross of his pastorate. He's often tempted just to let the youth program die.

Solo pastors' frustrations—Each small church pastor has a different relationship to youth ministry. Some are heavily involved. Others have a strong core of volunteers who run an effective youth ministry program. Others fumble along, trying to create an effective ministry they don't enjoy. Yet most share common frustrations. These include:

• Guilt—Pastors in small churches wish all their church ministries could be strong and effective. They know each ministry is important. They would like to spend more time visiting prospective families, checking on shut-ins, preparing sermons, teaching classes, planning youth group programs, counseling church members and taking care of all the other areas of pastoral ministry.

But they can't—as hard as they may try.

So unless they're careful, guilt sets in. Guilt when a sermon falls flat. Guilt when a program isn't polished. Guilt when they don't have the skills or resources to deal with a crisis. Guilt when they can't find ways to attract kids to the church's youth program.

• Lack of interest in youth ministry—If a pastor doesn't feel called to youth ministry, the responsibility can be frustrating and draining.

Juan found himself in this situation. He first felt called to ministry. He believed the Bible called the church to be a servant, so he continually challenged the congregation to reach out to others.

His emphasis was deeply appreciated in his small congregation. Dedicated members felt challenged and nourished by his leadership.

At least most of them did. Somehow he could never get through to the teenagers. They were good kids, but he always felt out of place in youth meetings. He didn't enjoy the crazy games they played, the water fights they initiated or the things they talked about. When he wanted to talk about the homeless problem in the neighborhood, they chatted about high school football rivalries.

• Lack of youth ministry knowledge—Maryanne loves kids, and she gets along well with them. But she feels like a conductor without an orchestra score when it comes to youth ministry. She stumbles through youth group meetings, unaware of how to interest and motivate kids. She feels inadequate when a teenage girl confides that she's sexually active.

Like Maryanne, many small church pastors feel unprepared for youth ministry, which can lead back to the first frustration: guilt.

● Lack of quality volunteers—Some small church pastors get stuck with youth ministry because no one else in the church will volunteer. And when someone does volunteer, he or she may not have the personality or skills necessary to run the program. So the pastor picks up the pieces.

Pastor's survival—A pastor who's responsible for shepherding the whole congregation can't devote a great deal of time to youth ministry. Here are some quick ideas to keep involved and up-to-date in youth ministry without burning yourself out.

● Develop a positive attitude toward youth ministry. Fostering a strong youth ministry doesn't require playing football, listening to Top 40 radio or being able to play the guitar. Rather, it involves creating an affirming atmosphere for young people.

In writing about the small church pastor's role in youth ministry, Joani Schultz argues that the pastor's attitude is the key to success. She writes:

> For two years, I traveled southern Minnesota as a resource person for church youth ministries. I quickly learned something about healthy youth ministry: the pastor's age means nothing. Attitude means everything. Where the pastor dislikes teenagers and sees no value in youth ministry, it shows. On the other hand, so does a tone of acceptance and support. I saw pastors, young and old, who cared about their *whole* congregation, including teens.[2]

Young people are a vital part of the congregation. By

developing a positive attitude toward kids and showing you care, you overcome many of the barriers that might otherwise make it difficult to reach young people.

• Address young people's needs in your sermons. Include high school illustrations kids can relate to. Preach sermons appropriate to their experiences—grades, family relationships, graduation, friendship, the future. In this way, you'll communicate awareness of young people, show them you care, and encourage the whole congregation to keep young people's needs in mind.

• Be yourself. Forget the stereotypes of the effective youth worker. Different people with different interests, backgrounds and skills can minister effectively with teenagers.

Discover ways you can use your own gifts and interests in working with kids. If your skills lie in counseling, help young people one to one with their concerns and problems. If you see yourself as an enabler, foster leadership skills in teenagers. If your main interests are preaching and teaching, accent your teaching role in youth ministry.

Of course, your own gifts won't address all aspects of a well-rounded program. So find people with other gifts to work with young people in areas you feel uncomfortable or ill-equipped.

Juan finally overcame his frustration with the youth group when he enlisted help from volunteers in the congregation who were particularly concerned about young people. They provided the activities and personal support the kids needed. And when the kids felt accepted and needed in the youth group, Juan helped them channel their energy into service to others.

• Pray for kids. Pray for one of your congregation's young people each week. Surprise that person with a phone call or note telling him or her what you're doing. Or post his or her name on a youth bulletin board as "prayer person of the week."

• Spend time with kids. Once a month, invite one young person to do something with you. Run errands, make hospital calls, go out for a soft drink after school, or do that young person's favorite extracurricular activity.

• Learn about youth ministry. Set aside at least 30 minutes each week to stay current on youth ministry resources and trends. The resource listing on page 164 is a good place to start.

Also, keep in touch with denominational and area happenings. Watch for opportunities to link your kids with other kids. Even if only one or two young people can participate—go!

• Affirm young people. Make a special effort to thank or affirm one young person each month. Tell kids you care. Watch for their involvement in church, school and work activities. Never let achievement go unnoticed. One small church newsletter has a regular column called "Cause for Applause." It celebrates people's achievements and thanks them for their work in the church.

• Be aware of your young people's gifts. Start a 3x5 card file of their interests and abilities. Refer to your file regularly, and use their gifts in the congregation whenever possible.

The Part-Time Youth Worker

When small churches hire youth workers, it's often for part-time ministry. Some part-time youth workers hold down other full-time jobs and lead the youth ministry as well. But more often, part-time youth workers are college or seminary students.

Part-time leaders' frustrations—Part-time youth ministry can be unusually challenging and frustrating—particularly if it's stacked on top of another job or a full school load. The frustrations include the following:

• Lack of time—There are only 168 hours in a week. Of that, 56 hours are (or should be) spent in bed. Another 45 hours are spent either in school or at work. That leaves only 67 hours. Seems like a lot until you add time spent driving, planning programs, attending meetings, counseling, building staff relationships and spending time with kids.

Then you have responsibilities at home—buying groceries, eating, taking a bath or shower, washing clothes, putting gas in the car, exercising. Add watching an occasional TV show, reading a magazine or book, or calling your parents or friends on the phone.

You're left with about two hours. An hour for your family. Thirty minutes for yourself. And 30 minutes for God. Maybe.

It can be overwhelming.

• Distance—Distance can be a frustrating obstacle to a student who's a part-time youth worker. It's rare to find a position across the street from your dorm or apartment. So more often than not, you spend time driving to and from your church.

The distance usually isn't a great inconvenience if you just have to go on weekends. But there's always an exception. A weeknight meeting that "we'd really like you to come to." Or a tragedy in the church. Or special programs.

Whatever the reason, distance requires time on the road. It also adds feelings of guilt when you can't be at the church for everything.

• Low finances—One reason people take part-time jobs is for the extra income. Yet part-time youth ministry rarely pays much. As a result, part-time leaders end up working hard and still worrying about finances.

• Lack of experience—Since most part-time youth workers are students, they don't have years of training and experience. The frustration comes either when they feel inadequate or un-prepared.

Al was a college junior and a weekend youth minister for a small church on Chicago's south side. In youth ministry classes, he took notes on how to organize a year of activities, create attractive publicity and thread a film projector. His grades indicated he was prepared for youth ministry.

However, on weekends he took a different set of notes. He soon discovered organized activities did little good for his urban teenagers, and the church didn't even have a film projec-tor. Al witnessed the grief of a mother who lost her son in a gang fight. He felt the sting of rejection from a girl strung out on crack. He counseled a school dropout who survived by stealing purses.

Somehow the idealistic solutions offered in his youth ministry classes never quite matched his weekend youth ministry. Al felt inadequate.

• Lack of continuity—Most part-time youth workers won't be in their positions long. When the semester ends or they graduate, they'll be looking for full-time work. As a result, they sometimes feel like lame ducks treading water—just keeping the program going until they leave. And they know they'll never see the long-term benefits of their ministry.

Part-time leader survival—How can part-time youth workers balance school (or work) and youth ministry? Here are several general principles to keep in mind:

• Set priorities. With limited time and energy, it's important to keep priorities in mind. What are your most important responsibilities?

Your first responsibility is to develop a growing relationship with God. Often our one-to-one time with God is the first thing we discard when time pressures mount. However, a deep relationship with Christ will be our rock in difficult times.

Second, if you're married, you're responsible to your family. Create times where you can be together. Go for walks. Plan a weekly getaway to a restaurant. If you have children, spend time with them.

Part-time youth workers who are single also have a responsibility to develop healthy personal relationships. While it may be tempting to rely on the youth group for social interaction, the group can never meet your need for intimacy with close friends your own age.

Youth workers who don't make friendships a priority find themselves burned out and empty. And they have no one with whom to share their deep, personal feelings, fears, joys and sorrows.

Third, you are responsible to your work or school. If your youth ministry is crowding out studies or cutting your effectiveness on the job, re-evaluate your church position. If you are in school full time, the education you receive today must last a lifetime.

Finally, you are also responsible to yourself. Eat right and get adequate sleep and exercise. Make time to rest. It's better to pace your ministry than to burn the candle at both ends and end up with only a puddle of wax.

• Learn time management. Time is a valuable commodity. Use the time management principles discussed in Chapter 9. Also block off at least 10 hours every week for yourself and your family (or other significant relationships, if you're single). It's not a lot to ask. And it's better to give the time now than to squeeze time in later trying to rebuild a marriage.

• Delegate. It's easy to be like the ancient Greek god Atlas in part-time youth ministry: You try to carry the whole world on your own shoulders. You have specific responsibilities to fulfill. And you're not around the church all the time, so it's easy just to do things yourself. And particularly if it's your first ministry position, you're anxious to make a good impression. So you do all the work.

But doing all the work doesn't help you or the church. You end up overloaded, and church members never learn how to lead the ministry. By delegating tasks, you help build the church for the future.

• Limit people's expectations. The church and youth group members need to understand you're part time—you have other responsibilities. Except for emergencies, young people need to turn to other adults for help when you're not around.

Adults need to be aware you won't be able to participate in every church function during the week. By making expectations clear in the beginning, you prevent hard feelings later on.

To keep expectations manageable, work with the church to develop a specific job description that spells out how much you can work, when you can work and when to make exceptions for emergencies. Then find one or two volunteer youth workers who are willing to help with specific needs that arise at other times.

Holly used this approach when she found her youth ministry position was jeopardizing her schoolwork. It seemed that whenever she had a major test in school, a teenager had some kind of crisis—a girlfriend broke up, a friend committed suicide, the teenager caught mono. Feeling her obligation to the kids, Holly would stop studying so she could help. Then she'd have to stay up all night to prepare for the test.

After a particularly difficult month in school and at church, Holly finally expressed her frustration to the pastor. The pastor suggested she find some good volunteers who could be on call when Holly needed to study. Holly talked with two adults the kids related to well, explained her situation and asked them to share in her ministry. They readily agreed.

Then Holly explained in the newsletter what she had done and why. She told who would be available on different days and published their phone numbers.

Now when something comes up at church while Holly is at school, the church office refers the person to the appropriate volunteer. Since the kids already feel close to the other adults, the transition has been smooth and effective. And Holly doesn't have to lose sleep because a youth group problem interrupted her studying.

The Full-Time Youth Worker

The full-time youth minister in a small church is a rarity. The full-time youth minister faces a unique set of frustrations and has unique opportunities for ministry.

Full-time leader's frustrations—The full-time youth minister in a small church doesn't have an easy job. The hours are just as long as in larger churches—perhaps even longer. And the demands are just as great. Some of the frustrations include the following:

• Low salaries—Low salaries are a constant concern among small church youth ministers. Because they often don't have strong financial bases, small churches often underpay full-time staff people. Low salaries are a primary reason many small church youth ministers eventually move to larger churches.

• Multiple responsibilities—As stated in Chapter 2, small churches reward generalists. So when a specialist—such as a youth minister—arrives, he or she quickly becomes a generalist.

Small church youth ministry is much more than youth ministry. It usually involves being Christian education director, choir director, Sunday school teacher, basketball coach, counselor, fill-in preacher, Bible scholar, committee representative and on and on. Small church youth workers wear many hats.

Being involved in many different ministries has its benefits—you're never bored, and you always have new things to learn. However, it's frustrating when you're constantly pulled away from youth ministry to do things you don't feel prepared to do.

• High expectations—Facing different people's expectations can be tough. Different people have different agendas. And the youth minister may be constantly compared to previous "successful" leaders.

Other people will expect the youth minister single-handedly to transform the youth program—and the church. You're the one with the education. You're the one with books on the shelf. You're the one with the experience. So you do the work. "That's why we hired you," one elderly deacon once chided me. "You're the youth minister!"

• Isolation—Since small churches can be close-knit, it's sometimes difficult to establish relationships within the membership. This isolation is compounded in rural areas by the limited opportunities in the community. "I'd have to drive 90 miles to go to a shopping mall," confessed one Kansas youth worker, "or 20 miles to take in a two-year-old movie."

• Status—The temptation to seek better job status in a larger church is ever present in small church youth ministry. For youth workers committed to small church ministry, remaining in a small church can become a dilemma. Youth ministry colleagues may pressure a small church youth minister to get a better job in a bigger church. Other problems might arise later in a career when prospective employers wonder "what was wrong with Sandra" that made her stay in small churches for so many years.

Full-time leader survival—While the frustrations may be great as a full-time youth minister in a small church, there are several ways to overcome them.

• Discuss your salary and needs. If money is a problem, address the issue. Ask the leaders if they could survive on your income without other sources (such as a farm). Ask for realistic increases that will provide a modest standard of living.

When negotiating your salary, keep in mind the incomes in the congregation—it would be hypocritical to ask a church to provide a substantially higher salary for its staff than any member receives.

• Learn to juggle. You'll never be a specialist in a small church. Fulfilling many roles is just part of the job. So enjoy learning and growing in different areas. You may discover whole new areas of interest.

At the same time, set limits on what you agree to do. Instead of doing all the work yourself, find other people who can share gifts in a particular area. By encouraging others to take new responsibilities, you ease your own load.

• Learn to live with expectations. The problem with expectations is they're so hard to change. Sometimes unrealistic expectations dissipate as congregation members see and begin appreciating your gifts. Discuss the issue with church leaders so they'll understand what you're doing and why. Regularly share your methods and goals with the congregation, and report the good news from the youth program. Do whatever you can to help the congregation "buy into" your priorities.

• Begin your ministry slowly. Small churches are less open to radical changes. And they accept outsiders less enthusiastically. So when you begin your ministry, don't expect to rush in and be accepted. Instead, take time to build important relationships before tampering with accepted programs. The "Starting on the Right Foot" box gives suggestions for establishing a healthy new youth ministry.

• Adjust your lifestyle. If the isolated rural life drives you crazy, discover creative ways to relax in the situation. One North Dakota youth minister started flying model airplanes on the wide open North Dakota prairie.

• Examine your gifts and calling. You'll always feel pressure to move to a larger church. It's important, then, to examine where you have gifts and where they can best be used.

If your skills lie mainly in personal relationships, a small church is likely to be the most comfortable place for you. But if

Starting on the Right Foot

Starting a new youth ministry is exciting and scary. In her article "Surviving the Hurdles of a New Job," Wendy Lewis gives six ways to launch a new youth ministry position.[3]

1. Time your arrival carefully. The best time to start a new ministry is in July or August. That gives one or two good months to get used to the job change before the school year.

2. Use numerous "ports of entry." Every church has several "ports of entry"—ways to get involved and recognized in the congregation. For a new small church youth minister, these might include making announcements, leading a Bible study or serving ice cream at an all-church social. Whatever ports you use, try as many ways as possible to get acquainted with church members.

3. Go for an early success. It's tempting to spend lots of time evaluating and analyzing. But it's better to jump right in with some short-term plans. The new church will be looking for you to make things happen. Put everyone at ease by doing something that's comfortable to the church—something that was a big success in the recent past. Don't radically change existing programs, but polish them or add new ideas that seem appropriate. One church with an apathetic youth group remembered one big success: a community walk for the hungry. So the new leader built on that enthusiasm, but added a world-hunger-awareness meal after the walk. The kids loved the event, and the youth worker gained credibility in the congregation.

4. Support the previous youth leader. Regardless of your predecessor's success or failure, don't turn him or her into a scapegoat. People will notice if you're critical of previous efforts, and you could lose their respect.

5. Introduce change gradually. It's tempting to try to give your new youth group an overnight face lift. But that can be a major mistake. It's important first to earn the right to be heard. Be patient. Change will come in its own time. To force it can create resistance and resentment.

6. Develop a positive relationship with the church leadership. Get to know church leaders through formal and informal occasions. Take advantage of lunch and dinner invitations. Find out church leaders' perceptions of the youth ministry as well as their dreams for its future. Remember the relationships you build now with the church leaders will be the relationships you'll rely on when times get difficult.

your gifts revolve around administration and organization, you may be better suited to work in a large church.

However, when considering a career move, examine your motives carefully. Many youth ministers leave small churches because of prestige and the desire to get away from the stresses. But they discover a whole new set of stresses in the larger church.

It takes unique gifts to work with a small church, just as it takes unique talents to direct a large church youth program. Knowing what you can or can't do will help you make better decisions concerning whether to stay or leave.

Common Goals

Each type of youth worker in the small church struggles with a different set of circumstances and frustrations. Your particular situation may be difficult. You may be a volunteer who has little training and few resources. You may be a pastor with youth ministry as one of scores of other responsibilities. You may be a part-time youth leader who squeezes youth work in with a demanding school load. Or you may be a full-time youth leader who spends your time juggling multiple responsibilities.

Regardless of your particular situation, you share common goals with other youth workers in small churches. You want to touch kids' lives. You want to challenge young people to dedicate themselves to Christ and his way of life. You want to see today's teenagers grow up to be tomorrow's leaders—in the church and the world.

And you can strive for those goals whatever your situation.

Endnotes

[1] Joani Schultz, "Good News for Volunteers!" Youth Leader's Digest (Fall/Winter 1986-87), 27.

[2] Joani Schultz, "How Small Churches Minister to Youth," Leadership Journal (Spring 1985), 80-81.

[3] Wendy Lewis, "Surviving the Hurdles of a New Job," GROUP Magazine (September 1987), 10-14.

CHAPTER 11

28 Activities for Small Churches

P rogramming ideas for youth groups fill bookstores and catalogs. But sometimes it's hard to find ideas that work with small groups in small churches. Sure, a lot of ideas are adaptable. But many either cost too much or require too many participants to be feasible in small churches.

This chapter gives some ideas for creative programming. None require more than eight or 10 kids. And none will bust your budget. They're divided into the following categories:

- Spiritual Growth;
- Fun and Fellowship;
- Affirmations; and
- Service Projects and Fund-Raisers.

Spiritual Growth

The Cube

Here's a share-and-care idea for small groups. Find a cube with the same dimensions on every side, such as a tall facial tissue box. Cover the cubes with plain gift wrap or construction

paper. Then write a share-and-care question on each side of
the box:

• What's one thing you appreciate about the person on
your right?

• How is God working in your life?

• What's your favorite Bible verse, and why?

• If you could change one area of your life, what would it
be?

• What's something you'd like the group to pray about?

• What do you like most about the youth group?

During youth group sharing times, have each person roll
the cube and answer the question on the top of the cube.

Motel Retreat

Often small youth groups have trouble finding retreat
locations. But your problem is solved by a nearby motel. For
the same cost a larger youth group might pay for a retreat center, you can secure rooms at any quality motel and still have
money left over! Find a motel with extras, such as an indoor
pool or whirlpool.

Motels make great retreat sites for small groups because
they have everything you need. If you need an extra meeting
area, most motels will provide one for a small charge.

Sitcom Situations

Most 30-minute TV sitcoms spend the first 15 minutes
setting up a situation or problem, such as losing a girlfriend or
being tempted to cheat. Then after a commercial break, the
sitcom solves the problem or difficult dilemma.

Here's a neat idea for a living room discussion. As a
group, watch the first half of a popular TV sitcom. Once the
situation or problem is developed, turn off the television and
give the group 15 minutes to discuss how to resolve the situation from a Christian perspective. Have each young person
role-play one of the major characters in the program based on
the resolution the group agreed to. If there are more characters
than you have group members, simply adapt the script.

Prayer Partners

Help group members learn to make prayer a part of their daily lives by having them choose an older church member as a prayer partner for a month. Have each pair get together weekly for a short devotional and prayer time. Then have people each pray for their partner through the week.

Youth Group Exchange

Learn about other cultures and church traditions by arranging a youth group exchange with another small congregation from a different tradition. If you serve a Hispanic church, exchange with a black, Chinese or Anglo congregation, or vice versa. Or if you're from a mainline church, exchange with an evangelical church, or vice versa.

On one Sunday, have your youth group visit the other church. Attend Sunday school and worship. Then have a meal together. In the afternoon, have a special youth group meeting that gives the flavor of the host church's approach. The next week, host the other youth group for a similar experience.

Gravestone Epitaphs

Visit a graveyard after dark (with permission from proper authorities) to help your young people understand about death and eternal life. Have kids read different epitaphs on the gravestones. Have them choose one epitaph and make a gravestone rubbing. Have them place newsprint over the face of the gravestone, and rub a crayon all over the newsprint.

Then sit in a clearing to read the epitaphs. Have kids imagine what the people were like. Ask them to think about how they'd like to be remembered, and have them write epitaphs for themselves. Conclude with a Bible study on death.

Paper Towers

This is a fun activity to help kids work together at problem-solving and dealing with failure. You can do the activity with just two kids.

Gather cellophane tape and 100 to 200 sheets of construction paper for every four kids. Have kids build a seven-foot-tall paper tower. The tower must be free-standing and must be able to hold a medium-size book for one minute. Teams can plan for two minutes, then they must work in silence.

After teams each have completed their tower, discuss how many times they failed, how they responded to the failures, and which kids took leadership roles. Have kids discuss biblical characters who failed and how they survived.

Fun and Fellowship

Living Room Concerts

You can't afford to sponsor Christian concerts, and you're reluctant to ask kids to shell out the admission fee to attend public concerts. So how do you introduce your group members to contemporary Christian music groups?

Bring the groups to them—in living color. Host monthly Christian music video nights, and feature different groups each time. You supply the drinks, and the kids bring munchies.

Check your Christian bookstore to see if it carries Christian music videos for group rental. If yours doesn't, ask the manager about other distributors.

Secret Destination

A favorite activity for many youth groups is Secret Destination. Cart off the kids someplace for fun and fellowship without telling anyone where you're going. You can go to a home for an evening of games. Roast marshmallows on someone's farm. Visit a local ice cream shop for sundaes. Or go bowling.

Make the activity even more crazy by blindfolding everyone before you leave (except the driver!). Make numerous twists and turns to confuse people. Have kids guess where you're going.

Progressive Fast-Food Dinner

Instead of a regular progressive dinner, have a progressive dinner at fast-food restaurants. Kids buy their own food. Check individual costs at each restaurant before going and tell kids how much money to bring.

Eat each course before going to the next restaurant. For example, begin at McDonalds with drinks, then head to Wendy's for a burger, followed by fries at Long John Silver's. Add an apple pie at Hardee's.

A twist is to write on a slip of paper each restaurant and its course. Combine the slips in a paper sack. Have a young person draw one slip to see where you head first (it might be Hardee's for dessert). Continue until you've eaten the whole meal—in an unusual order.

If you're in a major city, use the same idea but go to different street vendors for each course.

Pingpong Soccer

If your kids seem long-winded, try this activity: Find a pingpong table without a net (or a similar-size table). Have the kids form two teams and stand around the edges of their side of the table. Then have each team try to blow a pingpong ball off the end of the table on the other team's side. No one can use hands or any body parts—except the lungs. And teams each must stay on their own side of the table. Play five-minute quarters with one-minute rests between.

Award points in one of two ways:

• one point for blowing the ball off either side of the table on the other team's half; and

• three points for blowing the ball directly off the other team's end.

"Smaller and Smaller" Scavenger Hunt

You've probably heard of "bigger and better" scavenger hunts. Teams start out with a small object and must trade it in the neighborhood for a larger one and so on.

This activity is just the opposite. Begin by giving each team a large object (such as a table), and award teams one point for each object they gather around the building that's smaller than the previous one. They can only use an object once, and all the objects must be neatly lined up from start to finish.

Allow 30 to 45 minutes for the scavenger hunt. Then award the winners with a crazy prize, such as a spray-painted gold garbage can. Give a second prize to the team that gets everything back to its proper place first—and in neat order.

Summer Pool "Swim-In" Movie

This is a great, inexpensive end-of-summer activity.

Reserve an outdoor swimming pool (or find a church member with one) and rent a Christian movie. Plan an evening of pool games, diving contests and lots of food.

Once the sun slips behind the horizon, spread a large sheet along one side of the pool as a projection screen. On the other side, place your projector (not too close to the pool!). Have kids grab their tubes and jump in the pool for a twilight movie under the stars.

Watch out, this activity may become an annual tradition!

Computer Tournaments

In today's high-tech world, many teenagers own computers. And they have programs with great games that require time and skill. Find games that require several players, and use them for youth group activity nights.

For example, some computer baseball games allow you to set up your own league and play your own games. Some programs even store statistics and standings. Play a 30-game season through the summer months, ending with your own World Series in October.

If golf is a favorite, check into various golf games. Most programs will allow up to four people to play golf on some of the best "courses" in the world.

Pizza Feast Scramble

Order a plain cheese pizza, and gather a pair of mittens, hat, scarf, fork, glass of soft drink with a straw and a die. Place all the items in the middle of a table, and serve a slice of pizza onto a plate. Then have each person roll the die. When someone rolls a six, he or she may start drinking the soft drink and eating the slice of pizza with the fork—but only after donning the mittens, hat and scarf, and circling the table once.

While the person is doing all this, the other group members—in turn—roll the die. The next person to roll a six stops the previous person from his or her pizza quest, and must continue the quest for pizza.

The winner is the person who swallows the last bite of the pizza slice and sucks the last of the soft drink through the straw. Award the winner the rest of the pizza (and pray he or she will share!).

Scrunch!

Form even teams of up to five kids and an adult sponsor (each team can be a pair). Arm each adult with an instant-print camera and film. Then have each team find as many places to "scrunch" into as possible. For example, a group of four might try to fit in the trunk of a car. Have the adult sponsor take a picture to prove the team did it. Award prizes to the team who scrunches into the most creative place, the smallest place, the most places, and so forth.

Nerf Ball Golf

Only about four or five kids can play this crazy golf game. You can play it at your church or in a home.

Create a crazy "golf course" through a home or church—down basement stairs, through cubbyholes, under chairs. Use small Nerf balls instead of golf balls, and brooms instead of clubs. Use shoe boxes as "holes," placing them in crazy places—in a tree, a stove, an open window (you don't want to overshoot!). Create holes that require bouncing the ball off walls and floors. Each shot counts as a point. Reward the person with the lowest score.

Another option is to use pingpong balls and plastic cups instead of Nerf balls and shoe boxes.

Bubble Makers

This is a fun summertime activity for all ages.

Before the activity, gather several quarter-inch dowels and a ball of medium-weight string. Using the following diagram, make several different patterns from the dowels and string.

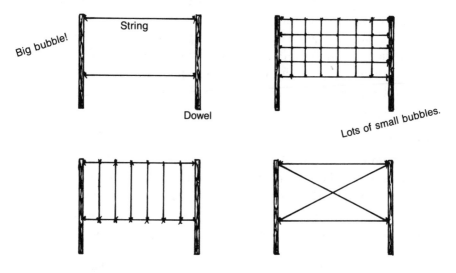

After you've created these "bubble makers," mix the following ingredients in a large container (a washtub works well):

● one part glycerin;

● two parts Dawn dishwashing detergent (this brand works best); and

● 10 parts water.

Have kids make bubbles by dipping their bubble maker into the "bubble water" and slowly hoisting it up into the air (allowing natural air movement to create a bubble).

Have a contest and see who can make the biggest bubble, the prettiest bubble, the bubble with most bubbles attached, the strangest bubble and so forth. Hold a bubble race to see whose bubble floats the farthest before bursting.

Affirmations

The Name Game

This fun living room game affirms all the kids at the same time. Give teenagers each a piece of paper and have them write their name at the top in large letters. Tell kids to have seven to 10 letters. If they have short names, have them use their middle or last name too. If they have long names, have them use shorter nicknames.

Then have a youth worker tape the names to the kids' backs. Tell group members to go around the room writing a positive trait about each person on his or her sheet, starting with any letter from that person's name. The activity is over when all the letters are used.

Great Graffiti

Celebrate group members' accomplishments with this great affirmation idea. Decorate a wall of your youth group room or a partition with newsprint, construction paper or even newspaper. Have kids each write their names—at regular intervals—with colorful markers.

Then have group members write affirming things about each other next to the appropriate name. Also attach any news clippings, snapshots and other memorabilia next to different names. During the month of a young person's birthday, attach a balloon and streamers near his or her name.

Weekly Care-a-Grams

A great way to stay in touch with all your group members is to pray daily for one or two kids, then send a personal note—at least once during the month—sharing how important they are to you. If you wish, call them to ask for specific prayer requests. Then encourage kids to share how things turned out.

The Love Chair

The love chair is a great way to have kids affirm each other. Simply place a chair in front of your group. Have one group member sit in the chair. Have group members each stand behind the seated person and say one reason the person is special. (It's sometimes easiest if you speak first.) Then have the seated person stand behind the chair and invite someone else to sit. Continue until everyone has been affirmed.

Service Projects and Fund-Raisers

"Somebody Washed My Windows" Service Project

Looking for a neat way to advertise your youth group? Put together a flier with a bold heading: "Somebody washed my windows!" Underneath write a little information about your church and youth group.

Then have your group head for the nearest mall, theater, community gathering or supermarket to wash car windows. When the windows are clean, slide one of your fliers under the wiper blade.

Caution your kids to do this activity with utmost care and courtesy. The last thing you want is an angry car owner.

Shut-In Shopping and Cleaning

This is a great idea any time of the year, but it's particularly nice during the Christmas season. With housecleaning supplies in hand, have your youth group visit your church's shut-ins and clean house for them—at no cost.

Group members might also prepare a grocery list with the shut-in and go to the store to buy needed food and personal items. Leave a couple of kids to visit with the shut-in so he or she won't think you're out the door forever with his or her money.

If you do this during the Christmas season, consider doing some of the shut-in's Christmas shopping.

Piggyback Fund-Raiser

If your group doesn't have the resources to organize its own fund-raisers, piggyback your fund-raising with other church fund-raisers. When adult groups sponsor dinners, serve and bus tables for a portion of the earnings. Sell concessions and run game booths at church social events. Or make and sell crafts for all-church craft fairs.

Pastor's Sidekick

Invite young people—one at a time—to accompany the pastor when he or she visits shut-ins. Beforehand, have the young people work together to write a short worship service for the shut-ins they each visit. They can listen to or sing hymns and say the Lord's Prayer together. After the service the young person can read to or write letters for the shut-in.

Generation Bridge

This activity not only helps kids learn more about their church and its history, but it also builds strong relationships between generations in the church.

Have the young people interview older members about their memories of church life. Find out how each person has contributed. Record the interviews on cassettes, and take pictures of the kids interviewing the older members. Then use the interviews and pictures to write newsletter articles, compile a church history scrapbook or hold an all-church party with the pictures and interviews as the main attraction.

Collected Thoughts

Have your youth group serve the church by creating a devotional booklet for a special season of the year, such as Advent, Lent, Easter or Pentecost. Have group members choose scripture passages and write devotional thoughts for each day. Also solicit poetry and meditations from church members.

Essential Lessons for Youth Ministry!

The 13 Most Important Bible Lessons for Teenagers

Ground your kids in the basics of the Christian faith! You'll use active learning to answer questions such as "Who is God?," "Who is Jesus?," and "What is the church?" PLUS: Step-by-step meeting plans, photocopiable handouts, and discussion questions are included!

ISBN 1-55945-261-7

Living Beyond Belief: 13 Bible Studies to Help Teenagers Experience God

These solid, in-depth Bible studies for youth ministry display how God's presence affected the lives of biblical people. As teenagers explore Sarah, Jacob, Ruth, Martha, Zacchaeus, and others, they'll see how God affects their everyday lives as well. Each 45- to 60-minute lesson includes active and interactive learning experiences, as well as worship time.

ISBN 0-7644-2099-9

Understanding God Together: 13 Bible Studies for Youth Ministry

Specially designed for small groups and small churches! These 13 dynamic meetings explore essential attributes of God and help kids see how those attributes touch their lives. Includes tips for adapting ideas to younger and older teenagers, and easy-to-use, photocopiable handouts.

ISBN 0-7644-2101-8

Faith on Fire: 15 Lessons to Help Teenagers Change the World

Debbie Gowensmith and Helen Turnbull

These innovative lessons show teenagers how to make a difference by caring for God's creation through community service and through global outreach. Plus, they'll see how the Bible applies to their everyday lives, in their community, and around the world. With practical help, fun activities, and action ideas, teenagers will be changing their world in no time!

ISBN 0-7644-2077-

Exciting Resources for Your Youth Ministry

At Risk: Bringing Hope to Hurting Teenagers

Dr. Scott Larson

Discover how to meet the needs of hurting teenagers with these practical suggestions, honest answers, and tools to help you evaluate your existing programs. Plus, you'll get real-life insights about what it takes to include kids others have left behind. If you believe the Gospel is for everyone, this book is for you! Includes a special introduction by Duffy Robbins and a foreword by Dean Borgman.

ISBN 0-7644-2091-7

All-Star Games From All-Star Youth Leaders

The ultimate game book—from the biggest names in youth ministry! All-time no-fail favorites from Wayne Rice, Les Christie, Rich Mullins, Tiger McLuen, Darrell Pearson, Dave Stone, Bart Campolo, Steve Fitzhugh, and 21 others! You get all the games you'll need for any situation. Plus, you get practical advice about how to design your own games and tricks for turning a *good* game into a *great* game!

ISBN 0-7644-2020-8

The Youth Worker's Encyclopedia of Bible-Teaching Ideas

Here are the most comprehensive idea books available for youth workers. With more than 365 creative ideas in each of these 400-page encyclopedias, there's at least one idea for every book of the Bible. You'll find ideas for retreats and overnighters...learning games...adventures...projects...affirmations... parties... prayers... music...devotions...skits...and more!

Old Testament	ISBN 1-55945-184-X
New Testament	ISBN 1-55945-183-1

Awesome Worship Services for Youth

These 12 complete worship services involve kids in 4 key elements of worship: celebration, reflection, symbolic action, and declaration of God's Truth. Flexible and dynamic services each last about an hour and will bring your group closer to God.

ISBN 0-7644-2057-7

Discover our full line of children's, youth, and adult ministry resourses at your local Christian bookstore, or write: Group Publishing, P.O. Box 485, Loveland, CO 80539. www.grouppublishing.com

More Resources for Your Youth Ministry

New Directions for Youth Ministry
Wayne Rice, Chap Clark and others

Discover ministry strategies and models that are working in *real* churches...with *real* kids. Readers get practical help evaluating what will work in their ministries and a candid look at the pros and cons of implementing each strategy.

ISBN 0-7644-2103-4

Hilarious Skits for Youth Ministry
Chris Chapman

Easy-to-act and fun-to-watch, these 8 youth group skits are guaranteed to get your kids laughing—and listening. These skits help your kids discover spiritual truths! They last from 5 to 15 minutes, so there's a skit to fit into any program!

ISBN 0-7644-2033-X

Character Counts!: 40 Youth Ministry Devotions From Extraordinary Christians
Karl Leuthauser

Inspire your kids, introduce them to authentic heroes, and help them celebrate their heritage of faith with these 40 youth ministry devotions from the lives of extraordinary Christians. These brief, interactive devotions provide powerful testimonies from faithful Christians like Corrie ten Boom, Mother Teresa, Dietrich Bonhoeffer, and Harriet Tubman. Men and women who lived their faith without compromise, demonstrated Christlike character, and whose true stories inspire teenagers to do the same!

ISBN 0-7644-2075-5

On-the-Edge Games for Youth Ministry
Karl Rohnke

Author Karl Rohnke is a recognized, established game guru, and he's packed this book with quality, cooperative, communication-building, brain-stretching, crowdbreaking, flexible, can't-wait-to-try-them games youth leaders love. Readers can tie in these games to Bible-learning opportunities or just play them.

ISBN 0-7644-2058-5

Discover our full line of children's, youth, and adult ministry resources at your local Christian bookstore, or write: Group Publishing, P.O. Box 485, Loveland, CO 80539. www.grouppublishing.com